The Story
of the
British Museum

Marjorie Caygill

UMETLD

Published for the Trustees of the British Museum
by British Museum Press

Photographic Acknowledgements

With the following exceptions the illustrations
have all been taken from material in the
collections of the British Museum: p. 63 ©
Associated Press; pp. 9, 17, 23 (lower right), 41
(bottom) British Library; p. 34 (top) Courtauld
Institute (photo by Geoffrey House); p. 27
(bottom right) Mrs E. M. James; p. 15 National
Portrait Gallery; p. 41 (top right) Society of
Antiquaries; p. 61 by kind permission of Giles
and the Daily Express; p. 62 courtesy of Mr
Alan F. Raymond.

© 1981 The Trustees of the British Museum
Reprinted 1985
Second Edition 1992
Reprinted, with revisions, 1996

Published by British Museum Press
A division of The British Museum Company Ltd
46 Bloomsbury Street, London WC1B 3QQ

British Library Cataloguing in Publication Data.
A catalogue record for this book is available from the
British Library.

ISBN 0 7141 1728 5

Designed by Norman Ball
Cover design by Bernard Friedman

Set in Monophoto Ehrhardt
and printed in Great Britain by
The Bath Press, Bath.

COVER: *The 'pigeon-haunted' Ionic Colonnade of the British
Museum, designed by Sir Robert Smirke. The great entrance
portico is eight columns in width. The entire front has 44
columns, five feet at their lower diameter, 45 feet high.*

It is a matter both for regret and for congratulation that the old British Museum is no more. It is no longer possible for the inquisitive visitor to Bloomsbury to see the 'cabinet of curiosities' in which a 'section of an old palace near Moscow' was displayed next to earthernware from Southern America, figures of German miners, Chinese and 'other Shoes'; where, before modern principles of classification imposed an element of uniformity, the model of a Chinese junk, bows and arrows and snow shoes were thought to be fit companions for King William and Queen Mary cut in walnut shells and a landscape painted on a spider's web, not to mention the jaw and other parts of an unknown animal from Maastricht, stones from the bladders of horses and hairballs from the stomachs of cows. In this 'huge labyrinthine lumber room' there lurked in the basements:

... monsters preserved in spirits ... which never ought on any account to be exposed to public view, lest the fancies of pregnant females might attribute to them the blemishes and misconformations of their future offspring ... Birds and other Animals in Spirits ... which from the length of the time they have remained in the collection and possibly from a failure of renewing the Spirits as they wasted by evaporation [are] no longer in a condition to be so prepared as to become a part of the collection of stuffed animals ...

The British Museum has the distinction of being the first national, public and secular museum in the world. Other collections, the Ashmolean in Oxford and the Louvre in Paris for example, were earlier but the British Museum was the only public

South-west corner of Montagu House, the old British Museum, from Great Russell Street, George Scharf the Elder, *c.* 1848–9. The sign on the fence exhorting the public to 'Commit No Nuisance' was erected at the request of the neighbours following a series of 'Indecencies'.

3

museum of any size which, following the principles laid down by Diderot and the encyclopaedists of the eighteenth century, had the temerity to aim at universality, belonged to the nation and, at least in theory, granted admission to all 'studious and curious persons'. Since its foundation in 1753 it has witnessed ten reigns, numbering among these sovereigns generous benefactors and four Trustees; it has experienced five royal jubilees, the first of which (George III's in 1809) necessitated a last minute lamplighter's bill of £56. 16s. 6d. for illuminating the Front Gate (an extravagance which the Trustees have not repeated). It has survived, more or less unscathed, numerous wars, revolutions and civil insurrections. The worst damage occurred in the air raids of 1940–1, but a potentially greater danger, the illicit smoking next to open barrels of ammunition by the Chelsea pensioners brought in to strengthen the guards during the Chartist demonstrations of 1848, was providentially averted.

In such a venerable institution the past is ever present. The so-called 'Botanical Staircase' has not changed its name in spite of the departure of the botanical collections to South Kensington in the 1880s. Other names which linger on are the Iron Age Gallery, damaged during the Second World War, which contains Renaissance and later material and the Maudslay Room (named after the great pioneer of Maya studies), where a Maya exhibition opened in 1922. No plaquettes are now to be seen in the Plaquette Room. 'Budge's Room', off the Mummy Room, was occupied by a Keeper of Egyptian and Assyrian Antiquities who retired in 1924. Hidden deep within the Museum are the Willoughby Stairs, named after a scaffolder whose office was located beneath them during his career in the Museum from 1931–53. (There is, however, a dearth of ghosts. An ex-Keeper is supposed to haunt the attics and a figure in butler's apron has from time to time been reported in the basements.)

On special occasions some of the warding staff still wear the Windsor uniform (granted by William IV in 1837) of a blue coat, with scarlet collar and cuff, with the words 'British Museum' engraved round the button. Although this was discarded by the Royal household during the time of the Prince Consort, the Museum continues to adhere to the style originally granted. A silver-headed mace, its origins unknown, bearing a hallmark for 1758 and engraved with the date on which the Museum first opened to the public – 15 January 1759 – is still ceremonially placed on the table when the Museum's Board of Trustees hold their regular meetings.

Time takes on a different dimension: headed notepaper bearing the Hanoverian arms was in use until the twentieth century; scholars work on series of catalogues first begun in the nineteenth century; a programme of baking one of the world's greatest collections of cuneiform tablets could continue for fifty more years, provided no more are acquired.

Although the British Museum no longer has the scope envisaged by its founders, having lost its natural history collections at the end of the nineteenth century and its great library in 1973, it is still perhaps the greatest museum in the world. It still aims to encompass the whole span of world culture. The titles of its remaining departments – Coins and Medals, Egyptian Antiquities, Ethnography, Greek and Roman Antiquities, Japanese Antiquities, Medieval and Later Antiquities, Oriental Antiquities, Prehistoric and Romano-British Antiquities, Prints and Drawings, Western Asiatic Antiquities – indicate just how wide.

The Museum may have the reputation of being a somewhat staid, conservative and ultra-respectable institution but its antecedents are less conventional, for it was established on the proceeds of a dubiously conducted state lottery. After the deduction

of expenses, £95,194. 8s. 2d. was raised by this means for the purchase of the Museum's founding collections and a suitable repository in which to house them. An undisclosed, but no doubt equally substantial, sum disappeared into the pocket of the swindler involved in operating the affair which, incidentally, is thought to have been the culminating scandal which helped eventually to put an end to the practice of parliamentary lotteries in the United Kingdom.

The 'father' of the British Museum was Sir Hans Sloane (1660–1753), a physician said to have been born at Killyleagh, County Down and graduated MD at Orange in 1683. Sloane's passion for collecting accelerated following his appointment as personal physician to the new Governor of Jamaica, the Duke of Albemarle, in 1687. On Sloane's return to London some time after the death of his patron he established one of the most successful medical practices in town, numbering among his patients Samuel Pepys and Queen Anne. He is also noted for promoting the practice of inoculation against smallpox and popularising the consumption of milk chocolate. In his house at 3 Bloomsbury Place, near the present Museum buildings, he amassed a vast collection of 'plants, fossils, minerals, zoological, anatomical and pathological specimens, antiquities and artificial curiosities, prints, drawings and coins, books and manuscripts' – so large, indeed, that it spilled over into the house next door. Sloane's house became a Mecca for the curious, among his visitors being Handel, who is said to have outraged his host by placing a buttered muffin on one of his rare books.

5

In 1743 Sloane moved his collection to his country mansion in Chelsea and there, in 1748, he was visited by the Prince and Princess of Wales. According to a report in the *London Magazine* Prince Frederick (father of George III), setting aside all formality:

... took a chair and sat down by the good old gentleman some time, when he expressed the great esteem and value he had for him personally and how much the learned world was obliged to him for his having collected such a vast Library of curious books and such immense treasures of the valuable and instructive productions of Nature and Art ...

The Royal couple were treated to a feast of 'drawers filled with all sorts of precious stones ... jewels polished and set after the modern fashion ... tables spread with gold and silver ores ... the lasting monuments of historical facts ... brilliant butterflies ... the remains of the antediluvian world ... large animals preserved in the skin ... curious and venerable antiquities of Egypt, Greece, Hetruria, Rome, Britain, and even America'. The Prince did not forego the opportunity of staking the nation's claim to this treasure house for he 'expressed the great pleasure it gave him to see so magnificent a collection in England, esteeming it an ornament to the nation; and his sentiments, how much it must conduce to the benefit of learning and how great an honour will redound to Britain to have it established for publick use to the latest posterity'.

Sloane died beside his beloved collection at the age of ninety-two and was laid to rest 'with great funeral pomp in his family vault at Chelsea'. He is commemorated in the churchyard of Chelsea Old Church by an imposing monument, an aedicula in the Palladian style executed in Portland stone, designed by Joseph Wilton.

Under the terms of his will his fantastic collection of 79,575 objects (not counting the plants in the herbarium and the library) was to be offered on two months' option in turn to King George II for the nation, the Royal Academies of Science in Paris, St Petersburg, Berlin and Madrid, for £20,000 payable to his two daughters – a considerable bargain since its collector had declared that it cost at least £100,000. Four executors and some sixty trustees were appointed to oversee Sloane's wishes. Thirty-four of these met at the manor house in Chelsea on Saturday, 27 January 1753, where the will was produced and read by Lord Cadogan. At a second meeting in the King's Arms Tavern a memorial to the King was approved.

This generous offer was received with something less than enthusiasm, the Earl of Macclesfield reporting back to an anxious meeting that the King had bluntly said 'that he doubted if there was money sufficient in the Exchequer'. The Trustees next tried their luck with Parliament through Mr Southwell, the Member for Bristol. Parliament was initially no more disposed to the acquisition of the collection. The general feeling of the House was that the proposal should lie on the table but, fearing that this 'would look like thro-ing cold water on the generous gift', they retreated, in true political fashion, into a committee to consider the matter further. Sloane's trustees returned to the attack with a list of 'Fundamental principles from which the Trustees do not think they can in Honor or conscience depart'. These were that the collection should be preserved entire, that it 'be kept for the use and benefit of the publick, who may have free access to view and peruse the same', and that if it were thought necessary to move the collection from Chelsea it should be deposited in the Cities of London or Westminster or their suburbs. James Empson, the curator of Sloane's Museum, appeared before the House to point out that the price was a bargain (his estimate of the cost was £80,000) and to assure MPs, rather optimistically, that on the basis of past experience it would cost a mere £500 annually to maintain. Horace Walpole was less complimentary, noting in a letter that 'Sir Hans Sloane valued his Museum at four score thousand [pounds], and so would anybody who loves hippopotamuses, sharks with one ear, and spiders as big as geese'.

Fortunately for the nation, Speaker Arthur Onslow was able to muster Parliamentary support and eventual agreement to a grand gesture that would cost the legislators nothing in hard cash. It was arranged that the collection would be purchased with the proceeds of a public lottery and in June 1753 George II gave his assent to the British Museum Act which, with relatively minor amendments, was to govern the affairs of the Museum until the passing of a new Act in 1963.

The Museum was fortunate in the new governing body of Trustees set up under the Act since it included, *ex officio*, some of the most influential men in the country. The three Principal Trustees, who were to take an active interest in the Museum's affairs, and who had authority to make all staff appointments (except that of the Principal Librarian, which was reserved for the Sovereign), were the Archbishop of Canterbury, the Lord Chancellor, and the Speaker of the House of Commons. These were assisted by twenty official Trustees – an impressive group comprising the Lord President of the Council, the First Lord of the Treasury (i.e. the Prime Minister), the Lord Privy Seal, the First Lord of the Admiralty, the principal Secretaries of State, the Lord Steward, the Lord Chamberlain, the Bishop of London, the Chancellor of the Exchequer, the Lord Chief Justice of England, the Master of the Rolls, the Lord Chief Justice of the Common Pleas, the Attorney-General, the President of the Royal Society, and the President of the Royal College of Physicians. There were in addition six (later nine) family Trustees; two representatives of each of the families responsible for the three founding collections – Sloane, Harley and Cotton (the three later additions were from the families of Townley, Knight and Elgin). Fifteen further Trustees were to be elected by the other twenty-six. These elected Trustees were to include over the years such famous names as Sir Robert Peel, Lord Macaulay, William Ewart Gladstone, Benjamin Disraeli, Baron Ferdinand James de Rothschild, Stanley Baldwin, Edward VII, George V and the Duke of Windsor (when Prince of Wales). A Trustee appointed by the sovereign was added in 1832 in recognition of the debt owed to the Royal family by the Museum. Other additions were the Presidents of the Royal Academy of Arts and the Society of Antiquaries.

The first meeting of the new Trustees took place at the Cockpit, Whitehall, on 11 December 1753 and was attended by the Archbishop of Canterbury, the Lord High Chancellor, the Duke of Portland, the Earl of Holderness, the Earl of Oxford, the Earl of Macclesfield, Lord Cadogan, the Speaker of the House of Commons, the Master of the Rolls, the Lord Chief Justice of the Common Pleas, the Attorney General, the Solicitor General, the President of the College of Physicians and Thomas Hart, Esq.

One of the first tasks of the new body was to discover a suitable repository for the collections entrusted to its care. In addition to Sloane's treasure house the Trustees had now to find a home for the Cottonian library, which included such magnificent items as the Lindisfarne Gospels, the manuscript of Beowulf, an important manuscript of the Anglo-Saxon Chronicle and two of the four extant copies of Magna Carta, as well as coins and other items. The collection had been formed by Sir Robert Bruce Cotton (1571–1631), Sir Thomas (1594–1662) and Sir John (1621–1701) and had been bequeathed to a less than grateful nation in 1700. The library had a high potential for

King George II painted for the Trustees, 1762, by John Shackleton (d.1769).

7

Montagu House was
originally designed by
Robert Hooke (1635–
1703), gutted by fire in
1686 and rebuilt to a
similar design.

survival; in spite of neglect it came through the dampness of the ancient and decaying family mansion at Westminster and later a fire at Ashburnham House in Little Dean's Yard during which the public were treated to the sight of the learned Dr Bentley in nightgown and great wig stalking out of the burning building with the priceless *Codex Alexandrinus* from the Royal Library, which was sharing the same dwelling, under his arm. Others of the charred and burning books came flying through the window. After these events the necessity imposed on the British Museum of looking after Sloane's collection provided the legislators with a heaven-sent opportunity of shuffling off another encumbrance. The third founding collection, the manuscripts brought together by the first and second Earls of Oxford, Robert (1661–1724) and Edward (1689–1741) Harley, was purchased for £10,000 from the lottery money.

The house-hunting Trustees considered a number of possibilities. The project of a new building in the Palace of Westminster was discarded on the grounds of expense – it would have cost £50,000–£60,000. Buckingham House (the core of what is now Buckingham Palace) was turned down on account of 'the greatness of the sum demanded for it [£30,000] [and] the inconvenience of the situation', although the vendor pointed out that it had 'cost the old Duke twice that Sum but Fifty Years Ago' and that 'Mr Timbrill the Builder who was allways reckoned an Honest able Man in his Profession valued it at more just four years ago'. The Trustees' choice settled on Montagu House, a fine but decaying seventeenth-century French-style house, possibly

8

by Puget, in Bloomsbury. Among its attractions were magnificent staterooms, a noble staircase, painted walls, $7\frac{1}{2}$ acres of garden, and its cost – a mere £10,000. The house had been empty for some time. Hatton's *New View of London*, 1708, describes it thus:

. . . an extraordinary noble and beautiful Palace, situate on the North side of Great Russell Street near Bloomsbury, in the occupation of his Grace the Duke of Montagu. It was erected, i.e. the Shell, in the year 1677. The Building constitutes three sides of a Quadrangle, it is composed of fine brick and stone rustick work, the roof covered with slate, and there is an Acroteria of four Figures in the Front, being the Four cardinal virtues. From the House the Gardens are Northward, where is a Fountain, a noble Terrass, a Gladiator, and several other statues. The inside is richly furnished; the floors of most Rooms finniered; there are great variety of noble Paintings, the Staircase and Cupolo room particularly curious, being Architecture done in Perspective, etc. and there are many notable things too numerous to insert here. On the south side of the Court opposite to the Mansion house is a spacious Piazza adorned with columns of the Ionick Order, as is the Portal in the middle of a regular and large Frontispiece towards the Street.

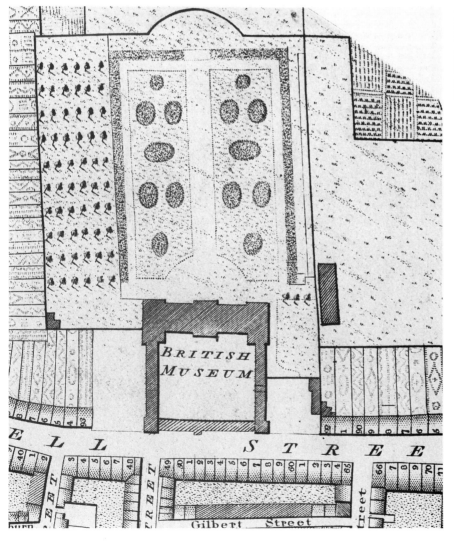

Montagu House and its surroundings, 1799. The fields north of the gardens were a favourite haunt of duellists, to the south is Great Russell Street.

By 1754 molehills spoilt the lawns and the structure was in need of attention; the Trustees little suspected that it would cost them £12,873 in repairs and alterations before it opened and this was to grow to £50,071. 14s. 10½d. by 1811. The Museum was, however, now in business and, although parts of its collections were many years later to be transferred elsewhere, the British Museum has remained in Bloomsbury on the same site to the present day. The great entrance and the old mansion have gone, but the impressive cast iron railings of 1852 parallel the line of the outer wall of the old house.

The Trustees now set about appointing staff and organising the collections, which were transferred to their new home between 1755 and 1759. In May 1756 they decided on a tripartite division, later to be rationalised into Printed Books (including prints), Manuscripts (including coins and drawings) and Everything Else, the latter more properly known as 'Natural and Artificial Productions'. Dr Gowin Knight (1713–72), a distinguished but somewhat irascible physician known for his invention of a new and

Gowin Knight MB FRS **(1713–72). The first Principal Librarian, a somewhat short-tempered man who disagreed with the Trustees over the payment of workmen's bills. His acid comments can be found in the archives.**

superior Machine Window Blind and an improved compass widely used in the Navy, was appointed Principal Librarian. Assisting him were three Under-Librarians, two of whom were doctors – Matthew Maty (1718–76) of whom Samuel Johnson said 'the little black dog, I'd throw him into the Thames' and Charles Morton 'a man of sedentary habits, extremely idle, disposed to let things run on from day to day and rarely to show the slightest initiative' (although three times married). James Empson, for many years curator of Sloane's collections, made up the complement of curatorial staff.

Bonds were signed by the new arrivals and placed in an iron chest (still in use today, although no longer for this purpose). Among the junior staff appointed were a porter (attired in a gown of 'plain drab colour with a yellow tuft' and bearing a black staff with a silver knob) who absconded shortly afterwards, four maids and a messenger. The new staff settled into their quarters – Dr Morton in the south part of the West Wing, Dr Maty in the north part of the East Wing, Mr Empson in the south part of the East Wing and the maid servants in the turret. One of the servants, Thomas Moore, was also consigned to the turret over the gateway where, following a plea to the Trustees, he was permitted the use of a specially constructed chimney on occasions of sickness or extraordinary damps.

The accommodation arrangements provided them, and subsequent generations of staff, with an excellent focus for their feuds. By 1768 the Trustees were having to issue an instruction:

. . . that all of them [the senior officers] in general should consider themselves, and the other officers, as gentlemen living under the same roof, and equally engaged in carrying on the same noble design, and among whom, for that, as well as for other reasons, no personal pique or animosity should ever find the least place; but the most perfect harmony and a true spirit of benevolence ought always to be cultivated and prevail.

Indeed, the suspicion is aroused from minutes of early Trustees' meetings that a large part of the staff's energies were taken up with defending and extending their territory and escaping as far as possible from the continually smoking chimneys.

While the installation of the collections progressed the Trustees decided to share with their neighbours the pleasures of their garden, in which they had placed many examples of exotic plants, some donated by the Duke of Argyle. One of their first appointments had been Mr Bramley, the gardener, who for £85 a year undertook 'Rolling, Mowing, Planting, Digging and Pruning'. Hives of bees were introduced in 1765.

From 1757 tickets were issued permitting holders to 'walk in the Gardens' provided they did not tread on the flower beds, pick or otherwise injure the plants or bring in dogs. This resolution of the Trustees was 'writ upon a painted board and fixed at the door of the garden' in 1761. That the privilege was greatly valued is evidenced by plaintive letters from visitors who fell foul of the Trustees by breaking the rules. One unfortunate husband, who complained that his wife had been rudely treated by an inferior female domestic who remonstrated with her for picking a pear, received the full fury of some of the mightiest in the land when the Trustees, far from dismissing their employee, withdrew the complainant's ticket and refused to reconsider their decision.

There is a tradition in the Museum that the Fleet River, or rather one of its tributaries, flows through the Museum site. Recent research has failed to corroborate this and certainly it is not shown on early plans of the garden.

The Encampment in the Museum Gardens, 5 August 1780. During the savage Gordon Riots of 1780 a contingent of the York Regiment of Militia was sent by forced march from Doncaster to protect the Museum and assist in controlling the London mob.

A less welcome group of visitors to the gardens were the six hundred soldiers of the York Regiment who camped there during the Gordon Riots of June 1780 to protect the Museum from the mob which had already destroyed Lord Mansfield's house in nearby Bloomsbury Square. The Principal Librarian, by then Dr Morton, prudently absented himself from the scene but the remaining Trustees and staff welcomed these intruders even to the extent of formally recording a resolution permitting the Officers to make use of the West Water Closet. The soldiers became a popular attraction, two young members of the Royal Family, the Prince of Wales and Prince Frederick, joining the admiring crowds. The regiment marched away in August 1780 leaving behind a bill for £580. 4s. 9¾d.

Select groups of visitors had been admitted to the Museum from the beginning, but it was found that their presence and that of the staff attempting to arrange the collections were incompatible and so this experiment was largely discontinued. On 15 January 1759, however, the British Museum opened its doors to those 'studious and curious persons' it was directed by Act of Parliament to admit. These first visitors, rather grudgingly allowed in only by ticket applied for from the Porter and granted with the approval of the Principal Librarian, were conducted rapidly round the

Admission Ticket. Such tickets were much prized due to the ever-lengthening waiting list.

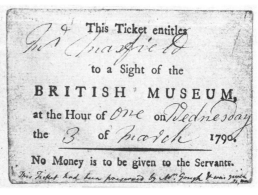

apartments in parties of five escorted by a member of staff and were not permitted to upset routine by gazing at the objects. The Museum was open daily (except Saturday, Sunday and various public holidays), usually from nine in the morning until three in the afternoon. On certain days in the summer this was altered to four in the afternoon till eight in the evening. The Trustees bent a little towards public opinion in 1761 when they gave up their attempt to restrict visitors to one hour per department regardless of their interests and magnanimously permitted each 'company' to decide democratically by a majority decision how they would spend their visit. Sub-groups were allowed to tarry behind the party under escort if their interest was caught, provided, of course, that they were out of the Museum in the allotted time.

An early VIP visitor was the Prince of Brunswick. The attraction of royalty was such that several persons succeeded in getting into the house and even forcing their way through the rooms, notwithstanding the endeavours of the Officers to prevent their intrusion.

A German visitor in 1782 described his visit thus:

I am sorry to say that it was the room, the glass-cases, the shelves . . . which I saw; not the museum itself, so rapidly were we hurried on through the departments . . . The gentleman who conducted us took little pains to conceal the contempt which he felt for my communications when he found it was only a German description [guide book] . . . which I had . . . So rapid a passage through a vast suite of rooms in little more than one hour of time, with opportunity to cast but one poor longing look of astonishment on all the vast treasures of nature, antiquity and literature, in the examination of which one might profitably spend years, confuses, stuns and overpowers the visitor.

Another visitor in 1785, who acquired his ticket from a tout (a professional dealer in museum tickets) for two shillings, was rushed through the Museum in thirty minutes flat. He writes:

I was not likely to forget Tuesday, December 7th, at eleven . . . We began to move pretty fast, when I asked with some surprise whether there were none to inform us what the curiosities were as we went on? A tall genteel young man in person, who seemed to be our conductor, replied with some warmth: 'What! Would you have me tell you everything in the Museum? How is it possible? Besides, are not the names written upon many of them?' I was much too humbled by this reply to utter another word . . . In about thirty minutes we finished our silent journey through the princely mansion, which could well have taken thirty days, I went out much about as wise as I went in, but with this severe reflection that, for fear of losing my chance, I had that morning abruptly torn myself from three gentlemen with whom I was engaged in an interesting conversation, had lost my breakfast, got wet to the skin, spent half-a-crown in coach-hire, paid two shillings for a ticket, [and] been hackneyed through the rooms with violence.

The Trustees had early considered charging for admission but in 1784 shelved this idea, having found to their regret that as those recently admitted to view the Museum had 'consisted chiefly of Mechanics and persons of the lower Classes, few of whom would probably have been at any expense to satisfy mere curiosity', the return to be expected 'would bear but small proportion to the defficiencies of the regular expenditure of the Museum'.

Simonds, in his *Journal of a Tour and Residence in Great Britain*, 1817, describes a tour which seems to have changed little since 1785:

. . . a German ciceroni took charge of us, and led us au pas de charge through a number of rooms full of stuffed birds and animals; – many of them seemingly in a state of decay. We had a glimpse of arms, dresses, and ornaments of savages hung around; – of a collection of minerals; – next of antiquities from Herculaneum and Pompeia and monstrous Egypt . . . We had no time allowed to examine any thing; our conductor pushed on without minding questions, or unable to answer them, but treating the company with double entendres and witticisms on various subjects of natural history, in a style of vulgarity and impudence which I should not have expected to have met in this place and in this country.

The Museum even at an early stage began to attract donations. As there was at first no regular government grant for purchases the Trustees were obliged to rely on the generosity of private donors or make special applications to Parliament. In February 1756 the first Egyptian mummy arrived at Bloomsbury – part of the collection bequeathed by Colonel William Lethieullier – and in June 1757 the Trustees acquired the magnificent gift from George II of the old Royal Library of the kings and queens of England. Founded in 1471 by Edward IV, it consisted of 12,000 volumes, among them Queen Mary's Psalter and the *Codex Alexandrinus* (a fifth-century manuscript of the Bible, a survivor of the fire which nearly destroyed the Cotton collection). With the Library came the privilege of copyright deposit (the right to a free copy of every work printed in the United Kingdom) – a privilege today vested in the British Library.

Some of the donations, as listed in the 'Book of Presents', were somewhat more eccentric: a hornet's nest found in Yorkshire, more compleat than are usually met with (1757); an entire electrical apparatus (1757); vertebra and other bones of a monstrous size supposed to be a large sea animal (1758); a limpet with a fish sticking to it (1758); the web of a silkworm wrought by the animal in the form of a ribband, with an attested narrative of the fact from the Viscountess Kilmurry (1759); part of the trunk of a tree gnawed asunder by the Beaver (1760); a stone resembling a petrified loaf (1760); the ear and tail of an elephant from Africa (1762); a starved cat and rat (1762); a piece of lace made of the hair of Queen Elizabeth (1762); a Chinese bowl disfigured by the fire occasioned by the earthquake at Lisbon and dug out of the ruins two years after; some nails dug from the ruins of the earthquake at Lisbon (1764); a live tortoise from North America (1765); a dried thumb dug up in the foundations of St James's Coffee House (1766); an unburnt brick taken out of the foundation of the supposed Tower of Babylon (1768); a basket made of cloves supposed to have been made about 200 years ago (1768); a chicken with two heads (1769); a pebble of the figure of a pear found in a field near Stonehenge (1769); a monstrous pig from Chalfont St Giles (1770).

More normal acquisitions came from Thomas Hollis whose collection of assorted antiquities from Italy and Sicily – 'small images in bronze, with a variety of instruments and other utensils: as likewise several marble inscriptions in Greek and Latin; with a considerable number of Etruscan vases, sacrificing vessels, lamps and some other articles' – was received in 1757.

Solomon Da Costa, the donor of a magnificent collection of Hebrew manuscripts, in a letter of 1760 to 'the honourable personages appointed and made overseers of the great and noted treasury called the British Museum' expresses the awe and respect which that institution was beginning to exert on the scholarly world:

. . . they have built a tower for them all [science and arts] and a palace full of all good things, the wonders of nature, which God created and made; and things of great value, both by reason of their being singular, there being no other like them, by reason of the costliness and beauty, or by

artists, whose fame has gone forth through the world. There are they deposited and there are they to be met with in thousands and ten thousands, where they will be for ever a sign and wonder and spacious rooms full of books, both modern and ancient, printed and manuscripts, in innumerable languages the like was not seen, in all the earth since the foundation thereof, till now that the men of government expended abundance of money to purchase them, and to gather them within the great treasury, that it might be for the good of mankind, both for the stranger, and for him that is born in the land . . .

From the three Pacific voyages made by Captain Cook between 1767 and 1779 came outstanding artefacts produced by the 'noble savage' and specimens of natural history (including, it is said, the first kangaroo to be seen in Europe). A magnificent barkcloth and pearl shell Tahitian mourner's dress is thought to have been given personally by Cook. Instrumental in obtaining many items for the Museum was Sir Joseph Banks, who accompanied Cook on his first voyage round the world in a vessel equipped at his own expense. Banks was later appointed a Trustee of the Museum and his generosity was commemorated by the installation on the great staircase in 1814 of a bronze bust – now to be seen in the King's Library. Meanwhile, these objects from the other side of the world were housed in a special room set aside by the Trustees in 1778 and papered with a neat mosaic pattern at a cost of £3. 12s. 6d.

In 1772 Sir William Hamilton, husband of Nelson's Emma, added to earlier gifts of volcanic specimens his collection of Greek vases. This first collection (the second went down off the Scillies in HMS *Colossus* in 1798 and was only partially recovered, in fragments, in the 1970s) was acquired with a special grant from Parliament of £8,410 plus £840 to be expended on a proper repository. Before this acquisition the Museum had not possessed classical antiquities of any consequence, now it began to grow into something more than a great library and natural history collection.

The great Shakespearean actor David Garrick bequeathed a magnificent collection of plays in 1779. With them came Roubiliac's statue of Shakespeare which was placed in the Entrance Hall and later in the centre of the King's Library. The statue was originally designed to adorn the temple to Shakespeare which Garrick had built in 1756 in the garden of his villa at Hampton. It cost him only £315 but the marble used for the head turned out to be riddled with blue veins said to have been likened to mulberry juice by the owner.

From the Reverend Clayton Mordaunt Cracherode the Museum received on his death in 1799 a very choice library of printed books, a cabinet of coins, medals and gems, a series of original drawings, including Dürers and Rembrandts chosen with exquisite taste, and a small but precious cabinet of minerals. Cracherode's quiet, retiring life – his farthest expedition from London was to Oxford – was darkened by the fear that he might, as holder of the (unvisited) manor of Great Wymondley, be obliged on the death of the sovereign to appear in public as the King's cupbearer at the succeeding coronation. His name was preserved in the Cracherode Room where his books were stored. There is a Museum story that when a member of staff committed suicide in this room by shooting himself his superior's first reaction was: 'Did he damage the book bindings?'

In 1802 a *'pierre de granite noir chargée de trois bandes de charactères hyeroglyphiques Grecs et Egyptiens trouvée à Rosette'* arrived in the Museum. This was the Rosetta Stone, the key to the hieroglyphic script of dynastic Egypt which had been discovered by the scholarly expedition accompanying Napoleon's military invasion of Egypt. When the French were defeated the stone and other antiquities became Crown property under the Treaty of Alexandria and were subsequently presented by George III. Included with the Rosetta Stone was the enormous sarcophagus of Nectanebo II of the 30th Dynasty (360–43 BC) which had been used as a public bath in Alexandria.

The Trustees received an unpleasant surprise in 1805 when a superb collection of classical antiquities which they had been expecting to receive was found to have been bequeathed initially to the donor's family by a codicil twelve days before his death. Charles Townley, a Trustee of the Museum, had put together an outstanding selection of antique sculpture in marble, bronze and terracotta, largely from excavations carried out in Italy in the years following 1767. Included in the collection were the well-known 'Discobolus', a Roman copy of a Greek bronze original, possibly the discus-thrower by Myron, and, Townley's favourite, the bust of a young woman, 'Clytie', sometimes identified as Antonia, daughter of Mark Antony and Octavia. Townley's collection had been one of the sights of London at his house in Park Street, Westminster, and had done much to form the classical taste of England. Fortunately a compromise was reached over the bequest since the family were unable to provide the repository specified in the will. Parliament 'cheerfully', it is said, produced £20,000 and as a further inducement the Townley family received a seat on the Board of Trustees in perpetuity. The coins and gems from the collection were acquired later.

The latter part of the eighteenth and the beginning of the nineteenth century were taken up by increasing worries concerning the state of repair of Montagu House and how, with a chronic shortage of money, to accommodate the rapidly growing collec-

In the earliest photograph of the British Museum, taken some time before 1845, the ghostly form of Montagu House can be discerned. (Possibly by Henry Fox Talbot who carried out photographic 'experiments' at the Museum in 1843.)

tions. Dry rot was first reported in 1766. The following year one of the weights in the clock fell through the floor of the Clock Room down on to the Colonnade and shattered one of the lamps fixed in the gateway. In 1780 the stone vases over the Colonnade had to be removed, one having fallen and damaged a gentleman's carriage. The Principal Librarian's wall collapsed in the great storm of January 1799.

In 1802 with the arrival of the antiquities from Alexandria the Trustees' thoughts had turned to the erection of a new building which would be somewhat more suitable than the sheds in the garden now housing large pieces of sculpture. A sub-committee was appointed consisting of Charles Townley, Sir Joseph Banks and Sir William Hamilton and they, working with the architect George Saunders, put forward plans for a new building to be erected near the north-west corner of Montagu House as the first section of a range of galleries extending northwards. Funds were granted by Parliament and work started in 1804. The plans were revised to cope with the Townley marbles and on 3 July 1808 the gallery, a suite of thirteen rooms also housing the Cracherode collection of gems, coins and medals, the Sloane and Cottonian coins and medals, the Sloane antiquities, the Hamilton vases and other miscellaneous antiquities was formally opened by Queen Charlotte accompanied by the Prince of Wales, the Dukes of Cumberland and Cambridge. On this occasion:

The Lord Steward sent a Glass Cup and Cover from St James's for the Queen to drink from (as was Her Majesty's custom). A Cook also came from St James's to prepare a Dish of Cutlets, etc. for Her Majesty. The rest of the Entertainment was prepared by a Confectioner in Bond Street; and served in the Great Saloon.

Townley Gallery. The statue of Discobolus (the discus-thrower) can be faintly seen at the far end of the Gallery.

With the application of more rigorous academic standards the Museum was becoming less of a cabinet of curiosities and the importance of the antiquities collections (previously an appendix of natural history) was at last recognised by the establishment in 1807 of a Department of Antiquities under the numismatist Taylor Combe (1774–1826). The glories of Greece and Rome had caught the aristocratic imagination and the Trustees were nothing if not aristocratic.

Somewhat to the Trustees' relief the medical and anatomical specimens, including the monsters, were transferred to the Hunterian Museum. More drastic methods were used by the Keepers of Natural History. 'Zoological rubbish' was buried or burned and it is reported that 'some persons in the neighbourhood complained and threatened with an action, because they thought the moths were introduced into their houses by

18

the cremations in the Museum gardens'. The attraction of the garden terraces and fragrant shrubberies of Montagu House was somewhat lessened 'when a pungent odour of burning snakes was their accompaniment'. The stronger the neighbours' complaints, 'the more apparent became the Keeper's attachment to his favourite cremations'.

A Keeper of Prints and Drawings, attached to the Antiquities Department, was appointed in 1808 in the aftermath of a series of thefts by one Robert Dighton, a caricaturist and etcher, who had insinuated himself into the good graces of the Keeper of Printed Books in whose department the prints were then kept. Over a period Dighton surreptitiously plundered the collection. The disappearances came to light only when a dealer, having bought a print from Dighton, turned up at the Museum to compare it with the Museum's copy. Most of the missing material was recovered and the Trustees took steps to tighten security. The Print Room was eventually established in 'a long narrow room, in the north-east of Montague House, above that containing the Towneley Marbles, approached by a separate stone staircase, leading to a small vestibule, in the centre of which was the Portland Vase . . .'

Print Room, Montagu House, George Cruikshank, 1828. John Thomas Smith, the Keeper, stands on the left eulogising a print which is in a portfolio before six connoisseurs, who pay great attention, while a lady is quietly turning over the leaves of a book of prints opposite.

In 1810 the purchase of Charles Greville's 'noble Cabinet of Minerals' gave the Museum world pre-eminence in this field. And still the antiquities continued to arrive. In 1815 the Centaurs, Lapiths, Greeks and Amazons from the Temple of Apollo at Bassae were acquired. These friezes had been excavated some years earlier by a party of adventurers and transported to Zante where, due largely to the efforts of the Prince Regent, they were bought at auction for the nation for 60,000 Spanish dollars. On their arrival in Bloomsbury an unwelcome bonus, a live scorpion, fortunately in a torpid state, was found in one of the fifty-one cases. The scorpion expired after only a few hours.

In 1813 Admiral Bligh of '*Bounty*' fame presented a slab of serpentine from New Holland; 1816 saw the arrival of the Elgin marbles. These were brought to England by the seventh Earl of Elgin who, appointed Ambassador at Constantinople in 1799, assembled a team of artists and architects at first charged with recording but later with preserving. Shocked at the destruction of the remains of classical Greece, Elgin obtained a licence from the Sultan, who then ruled the area, to remove 'any pieces of stone with inscriptions or figures thereon'. He himself visited Athens briefly during a four months' tour of Greece and the work was largely carried out under an Italian employee, Lusieri. By the beginning of 1804 Lusieri had removed all the sculpture he

could without endangering the fabric of the building – 247 feet of the original 524 feet of the frieze, 14 of the 92 metopes, 17 pedimental figures, a Caryatid and column from the Erechtheum, four slabs of the frieze of the Temple of Victory, the statue of Dionysus from the monument of Thrasyllus and a number of Greek reliefs and fragments from Mycenae. The expedition also took moulds of sections which were not removed and casts taken from these, which remain in the British Museum's collections, are in many cases the only record of sections later destroyed or damaged beyond recognition.

The first sculptures arrived in England in 1802 and the rest somewhat later, having survived a shipwreck in the Mediterranean. They were first shown in a shed behind a house leased by Elgin in Park Lane. Although a revelation to many, they were not to the taste of others, particularly the general public and some of the Museum Trustees. The views of the majority were summed up by Cruikshank's cartoon 'The Elgin marbles: or John Bull buying stones at a time his numerous family want bread'. After a complicated series of negotiations they were bought for the nation in 1816 on the recommendation of a Parliamentary Select Committee. The price of £35,000 was considered by Elgin to be no more than half the amount he had spent on their acquisition. On their arrival in the Museum the marbles were housed in the grandly named 'temporary Elgin Gallery', in reality a large prefabricated shed built in the Museum grounds.

The public, or at least Cruikshank, were no better pleased with the fruits of British exploration. An 1819 cartoon shows a procession bearing a polar bear, a barrel of red snow and worms found in the intestines of a seal towards Montagu House while the Museum's curators are seen dancing in anticipation on the parapet. This did not debar Captain (later Sir Edward) Parry from donating in 1824 'dresses and implements of Esquimaux, various dried Arctic plants, six skins of quadrupeds, and thirty Birds, with some eggs' from his second Polar voyage. The polar bears considerably boosted attendances.

Meanwhile in Egypt Henry Salt, the Consul General, and his agent Giovanni Belzoni (a one-time circus strongman and hydraulic specialist) were putting together an exceptional collection of colossal sculpture which included the head of Ramesses II (then known as the younger Memnon), a head and arm identified as coming from a massive statue of Tuthmosis III (Thothmes), six seated statues of the goddess Sekhmet from the temple of Mut in Asher and a black granite seated statue of Amenophis III. (Belzoni's name can be seen today, carved by him, on the latter.) Salt, encouraged by Sir Joseph Banks, had fallen under the misapprehension that the Trustees wished to acquire the antiquities he collected and in 1819 a selection was offered to the Museum. The Trustees, brought up in the classical tradition of Greece and Rome, evinced a certain lack of enthusiasm. After considerable argument these superb sculptures were acquired for £2,000, the Trustees refusing to the last to take a sarcophagus which eventually found a home in the Sir John Soane Museum.

With the Payne Knight bequest of books, bronzes, coins and drawings (including one of the finest Claude Lorrain collections in existence) the Museum, 'rich in certain classes of archaeology', 'came to the front in all'. The first Keeper of Antiquities,

Landing the Treasures, or Results of the Polar Expedition !!!

Museum staff and Trustees dance in anticipation on the parapet of Montagu House as Polar treasures from Sir John Ross's expedition to Baffin Bay are unloaded. John Bull (left) is still unimpressed. Cartoon by George Cruikshank, 1819.

Moving the head of Ramesses II to the new Egyptian Sculpture Gallery in 1834. The operation was carried out by the Royal Artillery under the supervision of Major Charles Cornwallis Dansey, a veteran of the Peninsular War and of Waterloo.

Taylor Combe, died in 1826 and was succeeded by Edward Hawkins, another numismatist, who remained head of the department for forty years, watching it develop into one of the greatest collections in the world.

However, overshadowing these acquisitions was an addition to the library. This was the 'King's Library', a collection of 65,250 volumes and 19,000 unbound tracts collected by George III to replace the 'Royal Library' given to the British Museum in 1757. There is some mystery regarding the circumstances of the donation of the King's Library. George IV needed more space in Buckingham Palace but in his letter to the Prime Minister announcing his gift to the nation he refers to a desire to pay tribute to the memory of his 'late revered and excellent Father'. A scurrilous story later printed in the *Quarterly Review* of December 1850, and possibly circulated by George IV's brother Frederick Duke of York, suggested that the King had intended selling the library to Alexander I of Russia but had only desisted when offered a secret payment

from Admiralty funds of £180,000. No supporting evidence for this can be found. At all events a Parliamentary Select Committee recommended that the library come to the British Museum and Parliament voted £40,000 for the construction of a suitable repository for this magnificent gift.

This room, still known as the King's Library, was the first completed section of the Museum building as it is today. The Trustees had decided on a programme of staggered expansion in 1802, which was now revised. The architect charged with this project was Robert Smirke (1781–1867), then attached to the Office of Works and already known for his design of the rebuilt Covent Garden Theatre and the Royal Mint. In February 1821 Smirke had recommended the erection of two parallel wings to the north of Montagu House.

The intention to expand the Museum did not meet with the approbation of all. 'Young Oldbuck' writing in *The Times* of 13 April 1822 complains 'in these times of general distress [of] so preposterous an intention of unnecessary expenditure of public money'. The gift of the King's Library, with the requirement of housing it, made Smirke's east wing a reality. Work started in 1823 on what was to become one of the finest and most sumptuous rooms in London. The Library, which was completed in 1827, is some 100 yards long, 41 feet wide and 30 feet high. The four central pillars of Aberdeen granite surmounted by Corinthian capitals of Derbyshire alabaster, 25 feet high, alone cost £2,400 after polishing. This was the first phase of the new Museum which was to take almost thirty years to complete at a cost of £800,000.

The first floor above the King's Library had originally been intended for a national gallery of paintings, the nucleus of which had been steadily accruing to the Trustees. However, with the purchase by the Government of the collection of John Julius Angerstein in 1824 a separate institution was decided on, one MP remarking that 'He did not like the idea of the great works of Raphael and Guido being placed in the same edifice with collections of animals and fossils'. The Trustees transferred their better oil paintings – including Rembrandts, Claudes, Rubenses etc. – to the new institution.

The King's generosity was further demonstrated by the presentation of a collection of coins from Buckingham House in 1825. In the same year the start of the Western Asiatic collection, 'a collection of manuscripts, medals and antiquities of various kinds

Sir Robert Smirke (1781–1867), architect of the new British Museum. Bust by E. H. Baily, 1828.

Tom and Bob in search of the Antique, 1822. The Elgin Marbles and other classical antiquities acquired by the British Museum had a significant effect on English taste.

BRITISH MUSEUM. *Tom and Bob in search of the Antique.*

London. Publ. by Jones & Co. April 27. 1822.

illustrative of the countries situated on the Euphrates and the Tigris', was purchased from the widow of Claudius James Rich, Resident at Baghdad, who had recently died of plague in Shiraz. These were placed on display in 'two glass tables', their significance being little appreciated at the time, for the focus of interest was still classical Greece.

To the consternation of many Trustees and staff the Museum was attracting a clientele from all classes of society and indeed, by 1810, the number of visitors had reached what was considered to be a staggering 120 a day. Pressure began to be exerted by the rising middle classes for improved access and for a more scientific and efficient

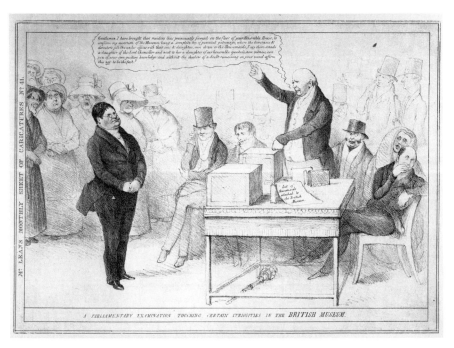

The cartoonist, inspired by Richard Cobbett's remarks in 1833, imagines the Principal Librarian Sir Henry Ellis before a Parliamentary Committee. In the background are the housemaids, 'daughters of the heads of the establishment'.

A PARLIAMENTARY EXAMINATION TOUCHING CERTAIN CURIOSITIES IN THE BRITISH MUSEUM.

Until 1837 the Museum's doors were closed on all public holidays. The sentry box occupied by the military guard is now swamped by the eager crowd. *Howitt's Journal*, 1847.

approach to the running of the Museum, or, as one MP put it: 'the public paid for the Museum and therefore had a right to insist on every facility of ingress'.

Richard Cobbett, Member of Parliament for Oldham, argued in 1833 that the £16,000 requested from Parliament for the running of the Museum could better be spent on starving weavers, especially the £1,000 set aside for 'cases of dead insects'. Somewhat carried away on the subject of nepotism, he demanded a list of the salaried persons at the Museum whom he suspected of being 'aristocratic fry'. The origins of the maids in particular should be scrutinised to see if they were 'daughters of the heads of the establishment'. The Museum's opponents cannot have been much appeased by the comments of the then Principal Librarian, Henry Ellis, who in a letter to a newspaper pointed out that the British Museum was 'maintained for many laudable purposes, among which the merely popular one of mingled amusement and instruction to those persons who walk through it is by no means the chief'.

One result of this agitation was the appointment of Parliamentary Select Committees which sat in 1835 and 1836. One of Ellis's more memorable exchanges with the Committee is the following:

ELLIS People of a higher grade would hardly wish to come to the Museum at the same time with sailors from the dock-yards and girls whom they might bring with them. I do not think such people would gain any improvement from the sight of our collections.

Q. Did you ever know of an instance of a sailor bringing a girl from the dock-yard?

ELLIS I never traced them to the dock-yards, but the class of people who would come at such times would be of a very low description.

There was a strong movement, however, which felt that gazing at curiosities might be preferable for the working classes than 'besotting themselves in public houses'. Among the Committee's eventual recommendations were that the collections should be split into more departments, staff salaries should be improved and outside employment by staff was forbidden.

On Easter Monday 1837 the Museum opened on its first public holiday. The building rapidly filled with 23,895 visitors, the most popular objects of attraction being

The Porter at the Entrance to Montagu House 'whose good humoured round face beams upon me even now, and whom I always thought a good embodiment of an Englishman, and a fitting introduction to the British Museum' (Cowtan).

Montagu House Courtyard by Shepperd. A large quadrangle bordered on the southern side by an Ionic Colonnade.

the birds, minerals, Mexican and Peruvian antiquities and Magna Carta. The Trustees noted that the pressure upon the floors of two or three rooms was very great and prudently called in their architect, Sir Robert Smirke, for an 'opinion as to their condition'. On Easter Monday 1841, 13,351 visitors turned up but, despite Ellis's misgivings, only two persons were refused admission on the grounds of intoxication.

What would the early nineteenth-century visitor see in his rapid transit round the developing Museum? On arrival in Great Russell Street he would find, as did a visitor in 1834, that:

. . . there is nothing to inform you what place it is. Some may, as there are sentinels at the door, consider it to be a barrack; then again, others may consider it to be some old, deserted castle, as the great and ponderous door seems not to have been painted for at least fifty years. Instead of there being a large board, or two, placed in front of the building informing the public when and at what times it is open, and what kind of persons are admissible, there is no information whatever – all is a dead blank.

At either side of the entrance was a sentry box with what appear to be, in some engravings, two rather bored soldiers leaning on rifles.

The guard was introduced in 1807 as a result of 'recent additions to the buildings and the new streets immediately surrounding it'. It came in extremely useful in 1815 when the Lord Chancellor's House – No. 6 Bedford Square – was attacked by a mob protesting against the Government's failure to repeal the Corn Laws. The mob, having torn up the railings and demolished the front door, raced through, only to be met by a corporal and four men from the Museum guard with fixed bayonets who arrived via the back door having been summoned by the Chancellor, Lord Eldon, who had evacuated his family to the comparative safety of the Museum. As the corporal and his men were successfully giving the impression of being a Company in single file the mob 'fled with great precipitation'.

Entrance Hall of Montagu House, George Scharf the Elder, August 1845. The staff wear Windsor uniforms, 'a blue coat, with scarlet collar and cuff'. Roubiliac's statue of Shakespeare is on the right.

Having passed the sentries the visitor then crossed a courtyard, 'worse than the middle of the street', where in bad weather he would get his feet wet. Once in the entrance hall he would, after the abolition of tickets in 1805, sign the visitors' book. After 1810 the Trustees permitted 'persons of decent appearance' to wander unescorted on certain days. Under this new arrangement a writer in the *Penny Magazine* of 1836 was found:

. . . standing in the entrance-hall of the Museum with his 'Synopsis' in his hand. The first thing that will strike his attention will probably be the words 'Ground Floor', under which is the following paragraph:

'This floor, consisting of sixteen rooms, contains the old library of printed books. Strangers are not admitted into these apartments, as the mere sight of the outside of books cannot convey either instruction or amusement . . .'

Our visitor might, however, console himself with a partial view through the upper part of a door in the Gallery of Antiquities. Having given up any attempt to penetrate the library he would find in the entrance hall and on the staircase leading to the upper rooms the bust of Sir Joseph Banks already alluded to, a statue of the celebrated sculptress Anne Seymour Damer (1749–1828) by Giuseppe Ceracchi (holding in her hands a small figure of the genius of the Thames – now at the north end of the King's Library), the Roubiliac Shakespeare, 'a gilt figure of Gaudma, a Burmese idol, presented by Captain Marryat [the novelist] . . . several preserved animals; a hippopotamus, a llama, a musk ox, a polar bear, an antelope, a Siberian elk, and three giraffes [one of which was the first, stuffed or live, to be seen in England]'. These objects were in 1817 already being described as 'seemingly in a state of decay'. Displays of manuscripts, medals and coins were situated in six rooms on the east side of the principal floor; Natural and Artificial Productions in the corresponding rooms on the west side. The visitor was recommended not to leave without seeing 'the sculptured tortoise, wrought in nephritic

George Byard, Senior Hall Porter, in Windsor uniform. Byard joined the Museum in 1827; the photograph was taken on the day of his retirement in 1867.

27

stone, which was found on the banks of the Jumna near Allahabad in Hindostan'. It is not surprising that Cobbett christened Montagu House 'the old curiosity shop'.

The 1830s were a time of change for both the building and the Departments. In 1836 the collection of prints and drawings was formally established as a separate department. The ethnographical and artificial curiosities, remaining with Natural History, were transferred to the Department of Antiquities. In 1840 Egyptian (but not Greek) papyri were transferred to the Department of Antiquities from the Department of Manuscripts.

In 1838 the Museum at last acquired a somewhat improved reading room in the North Wing. This had the benefit of central heating (a Perkins hot water apparatus), of which Smirke was a pioneer. This innovation was accused, however, of making a reader's head very heavy and his feet very cold and providing an ideal breeding ground for a creature known as the Museum flea, '*Pulex Mus.Brit.Max.*', larger than any to be found elsewhere except in the receiving room of a workhouse. According to an indignant letter in a newspaper, one member of the public celebrated the opening by removing one of the inkstands, 'first gracefully pouring its contents on the desk and floor, and then decamped with it in his pocket'. It was, however, a great improvement on the first reading room opened in 1759 – a narrow dark room with only two windows (which rattled in the wind), the floor covered with rush matting and the general air of gloom enhanced by cases of stuffed birds which lined the walls. The second opened in 1774. A third larger and more commodious room was provided in 1803. This proved inadequate and more rooms were brought into use. These were better, having 'long tables, with stands for reading and writing, at which sat many pale, cadaverous

Shaping the Portland stone columns for the Colonnade, George Scharf the Elder, *c.* 1845. These are Ionic in style with an Attic base.

personages, poring intently over dusty volumes, rummaging among mouldy manuscripts, and taking copious notes of their contents'.

By 1836 the room, now in the east wing, included a few 'idlers or triflers, who may be seen wasting their time of a forenoon reading novels or criticising the appearance or habits of their neighbours around them'. If the room changed the clientele did not. *The Times* noted sarcastically in 1854 that there were

... three to four hundred persons of all descriptions, among whom the shabby genteel greatly preponderate. Some fifty or sixty of these are employed in making extracts from encyclopaedias and books of reference; some two hundred and fifty are reading novels and the remainder are employed in looking at prints. Among the crowd are generally to be found a lunatic or two, sent there by his relatives to keep him out of mischief.

In 1842 the Lycian marbles, the tombs and other memorials of the Kings of Lycia, began arriving. (A reconstruction of part of the largest of these, the Nereid monument, can be seen today.) The marbles had been discovered by Charles Fellows in 1839 and were removed by the Admiralty under his supervision. Fellows was grudgingly allowed some of his expenses. The Trustees were horrified at the initiative of the Keeper of Antiquities, Edward Hawkins, who approached the Treasury for financial assistance. They obtained their revenge by imposing on Hawkins an artistic adviser, Richard Westmacott, who determinedly arranged the antiquities in their galleries in an artistic fashion with almost complete disregard of their antecedents. As the 1849 Royal Commission put it, 'very interesting parts of them [the Lycian marbles] are beyond the reach of observation, except with the assistance of ladders'.

Between 1844 and 1849 the officers' houses were built (the two wings extending south from each end of the Colonnade). Although all except one are now used for offices they are still referred to as 'Residences'. From the foundation senior staff had to live on the premises, a situation in which feuding and backbiting amongst them flourished. (This obligation was not dropped until the 1920s). The building developed piecemeal as, indeed, did the collections. The western galleries were begun but could not be completed until after the demolition of the new gallery of antiquities, the Townley Gallery, in 1846.

In February 1845 the Portland Vase, one of the Museum's greatest treasures (at that time, to the Trustees' embarrassment, on loan) was reduced to more than two hundred fragments by a young man using a conveniently placed 'inscribed stone of considerable weight'. The culprit, who claimed he was suffering from the after-effects of intemperance, was arrested and taken to Bow Street Police Station. Subsequently, before the Magistrate, doubt was expressed that he could properly be convicted under the Wilful Damage Act of the destruction of an object worth more than £5. The difficulty was resolved by his being found guilty of breaking the £3 glass case surrounding the vase and he was sentenced to a fine of £3 or two months' hard labour in the house of correction at Clerkenwell. In the meantime, as a result of careful work by the Museum's restorer, Mr Doubleday, the vase soon returned to exhibition. (The vase remained on loan for the rest of the century and was not bought by the Museum until 1945, with the aid of funds bequeathed by James Rose Vallentin.)

The mid-nineteenth century saw the emergence of interest in the biblical antiquities of the Middle East. In Denmark the foundations of prehistoric archaeology and of archaeology as a reputable academic discipline had been laid.

The Portland Vase, smashed by a deranged Irishman in 1845. The vase was taken apart in 1948–9 and reconstituted and again repaired using modern techniques in 1988–9.

The arrival of one of the colossal human-headed lions from Nimrud in 1852. This is probably the winged lion (Registration no. 118802) now on exhibition in the Assyrian Transept.

The first of the great stone sculptures to arrive from the excavations carried out during 1845–7 by Sir Austin Henry Layard at the ruins of Nimrud (which he then thought to be the site of Nineveh) were the great winged bull and one of the lions now in the Nimrud Central Saloon. On uncovering the lion, now in the Assyrian Transept, in 1846 Layard wrote: 'I shall not myself easily forget this enormous head appearing from the earth . . . like some giant arising from the lower regions'. The following year the bull and a human-headed lion, each weighing over ten tons, began their journey to Bloomsbury by raft down the Tigris. The party with the bull was attacked en route by a band of robbers and a mark on the stone made by a musket ball during the skirmish is still visible today. On Layard's second expedition (1849–51), funded by the Trustees of the British Museum, the King's Library of Ashurbanipal was unearthed at Kuyunjik. Three years later Hormuzd Rassam, Layard's assistant, discovered a further portion of the library which brought the total to some 25,000 whole and fragmentary cuneiform tablets. This find laid the cornerstone of Assyriology. Layard's discoveries caught the public imagination and an abridged version of his account of the excavation, *Nineveh and its Remains*, enjoyed an extensive sale in numerous editions, particularly at railway station bookshops. Layard's work was continued by Hormuzd Rassam, who was responsible for the acquisition of the great lion hunt of Ashurbanipal. Rassam operated for some time under the direction of Sir Henry Rawlinson, who supervised British Museum excavations in Mesopotamia between 1851 and 1855 and whose study of the trilingual inscriptions at Behistun contributed so much to the decipherment of cuneiform.

This interest in classical and biblical antiquities did not, so far as the Trustees were concerned, extend to other areas. By 1850 all the antiquities of ancient Britain and Gaul could be collected in four cases in one room, with a mere thirteen more cases for later British and Medieval antiquities. Even as late as 1870 a 391 page guide, *A Handy-Book of the British Museum*, covered the Celtic, Roman and Saxon collections in 6 pages, the prehistoric and ethnographic collections in 3 pages, the Medieval collection and Coins and Medals in 8 pages each. This compared with 80 for Assyrian antiquities, 144 on Egyptian and 129 on classical.

In 1845 Robert Smirke left the Museum and the task of completing the buildings was delegated to his younger brother Sydney Smirke (1798–1877). The last

Photograph of the demolition of Montagu House gateway, 1847. As further sections of Smirke's building were completed the old house was demolished by stages.

of 'poor condemned' Montagu House was demolished in 1845. The new entrance hall was opened in 1847 and the great south front of what is still the largest classical building in the British Isles was finally finished in 1848, the main gates and forecourt were completed and opened to the public on 31 May 1852. Also taking a hand was Sydney's son, Sydney junior, who was responsible for the lion's head fountains at each side of the main entrance door.

The new neo-classical Ionic facade was not to the taste of all. *The Builder* commented scathingly:

. . . we are not in love with – we are not thoroughly pleased with – the exterior character which Sir Robert has given to his building, we will say, without knowing him, that there is more of hypocrisy in it than there is in himself; it is a mannerism of times recent and times present; it is a bastard product of classic fancy, a false face (though a fair one) put on a noble carcase.

Lion-headed drinking fountains executed in white marble, 1859. The design is a repetition of that on the main doors alongside.

The Principal Entrance,
1851. During the year of
the Great Exhibition 2½
million visitors came to
the Museum.

33

Westmacott's pediment (***detail***). 'Man is represented emerging from a rude savage state through the influence of Religion . . . the whole composition terminating with Natural History, in which such objects or specimens only are represented as could be made most effective in Sculpture'.

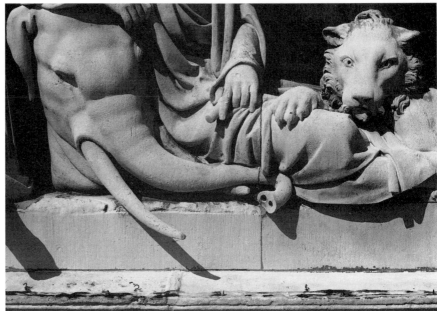

Cast-iron lion by Alfred Stevens which once surmounted the outer boundary railing of the British Museum. The figure, said to be modelled on a domestic cat, is the original of those now widely found on walls and gateposts throughout Britain.

However, the building won the Royal Institute of British Architects' Gold Medal in 1853. Mordaunt Crook in his history of the Museum buildings pays tribute to Smirke's design as a 'magnificent essay in the adaptation and integration of antique sources', 'the high water mark of the English Greek Revival'. The pediment above the main entrance was designed by Sir Richard Westmacott on the theme (illustrated from left to right) of 'The Progress of Civilization'. It had also been hoped to place sculptures by Westmacott (Shakespeare, Bacon, Milton and Newton) on pedestals between the iron railings and on the gate keepers' granite lodges. These, however, remain unencumbered awaiting suitable residents.

The boundary of the Trustees' property extended beyond the new railings and therefore Sydney Smirke commissioned from the sculptor Alfred Stevens a set of cast-iron lions one foot high on a four-inch base to guard the outer limits of the Trustees' domain. Stevens, faced with the difficult problem of fitting a lion on to four inches, is said to have cheated and used as a model the domestic cat of a friend. The little lions stood guard until 1896 when they were removed to allow improvements to be made to the pavements in Great Russell Street. That same year casts of the lions were put on sale and therefore copies of these elegant cats abound. Twelve of the originals can now be seen around Stevens's Wellington Monument in St Paul's Cathedral. Four are preserved in the Museum's Board Room. (Representations of the lions are now engraved on the glass entrance doors to the Museum.)

The middle years of the nineteenth century were dominated by one of the Museum's greatest figures – Antonio Panizzi (1797–1879), Principal Librarian from 1856–66. Panizzi was an exceptional man; he was born in the Duchy of Modena in 1797, and was forced to flee because of his involvement in revolutionary activities and arrived in England in 1823 penniless and scarcely speaking a word of the language. He possessed the dubious honour of having been sentenced to death in his absence and executed in effigy by the authorities. By industry, charm and the acquisition of influential friends he progressed up the academic and social ladder. Having joined the British Museum in

1831 as an extra assistant, Panizzi was appointed Keeper of Printed Books in 1837 and began a determined programme to expand the library both by purchase and by strictly enforcing the copyright acts. As a result of his activities the printed books collection had risen from 235,000 in 1838 to 435,000 in 1848 and 520,000 on his retirement adding volumes at a rate of 30,000 a year.

Panizzi shone before the Royal Commission of 1849–50 on the British Museum which was appointed to enquire 'in what manner that National Institution may be made most effective for the advancement of Literature, Science and the Arts'. Among other findings the Commission called in their report for a 'more prompt and vigorous system of management'. They advocated the formation of a national collection of British Antiquities and criticised the shortage of money for building.

One of the results of the Royal Commission was the removal of the then Museum Secretary, Josiah Forshall, whose tenure of the post had such a traumatic effect on the Museum's administration that it was not until 1926 that another Secretary was appointed. Forshall appears to have suffered from something of a power complex. He effectively ousted the Principal Librarian, the amiable scholar Sir Henry Ellis. He alone knew the proposed agenda of Trustees' meetings beforehand and could arrange it, adding or deleting items as he pleased. He attended the meetings, read such extracts from Keepers' Reports as he thought necessary to the Board and conveyed such information back as he thought wise.

It was to Panizzi that the staff owed the introduction of pensions and of conditions of service comparable to those in the Civil Service. Previously, unless they had substantial private means they had been obliged to work until they dropped, were removed to an asylum or to the care of friends or relatives. The Trustees might, at their discretion, award pensions but staff, such as the housemaid Sarah Griffin, might still

The Egyptian Room, 1847. 'Here, as everywhere else, last of all comes death' (contemporary newspaper).

be in harness at the age of seventy-nine. The Principal Librarian Henry Ellis started work at the British Museum at the age of twenty-three in 1800 and was still there fifty-six years later, retiring only when the Trustees agreed to continue payment of his salary. The Museum was also used as a last refuge for the more decrepit servants of the Trustees who had perhaps dropped the port once too often. Indeed, as late as the end of the century one Director still reckoned that one of his functions was 'to find soft berths for Butlers of the Principal Trustees'. A later not very strong candidate for Jack the Ripper was recommended by his doctors in 1875 'to retire from the British Museum before it is too late'. Jacquetta Hawkes in 1962 remarked of the staff 'it is wonderful that so many of them succeed in maintaining the British Museum's great reputation – also that more of them have not gone mad'.

Robert Smirke's original conception of the Museum had included a spacious quadrangle in which visitors might walk and admire the surrounding architecture (the mouldings are particularly fine) and which could be used as a garden. Unfortunately reality did not coincide with theory. The air did not circulate and the grass never looked very green as the surrounding buildings excluded the necessary sunlight. The quadrangle was therefore not opened to visitors and remained visible only through a glazed panel in a door in the entrance hall. The proposals for a reading room and book-stacks in this space were first put to the Trustees by Panizzi in 1852. The plans were refined by Sydney Smirke, and work on a single-domed circular reading room started in 1854. The building was completed in 1857 at a cost of £150,000 and the opening on 5 May was marked by a formal champagne breakfast ceremonially eaten off the catalogue desks. When it was opened to the public between 8 and 16 May 62,041

Photograph of the construction of the Reading Room, *c.* 1855. Upwards of 2,000 tons of iron were used.

visitors came to marvel. The Reading Room has a capacity of some $1\frac{1}{4}$ million cubic feet, a diameter of 140 feet (St Paul's Cathedral has only 112 feet) and the dome is carried entirely on cast-iron ribs. While *The Publishers' Circular* praised it as 'a circular temple of marvellous dimensions, rich in blue, and white, and gold', Panizzi's great rival the Keeper of Manuscripts, Frederic Madden, predictably snarled that it was 'perfectly unsuited to its purpose and an example of reckless extravagance occasioned through the undue influence of a foreigner'. Smirke intended that the room should be decorated with paintings, and an artist, Alfred Stevens, was commissioned. However, due to lack of money and Stevens's inability to complete anything, a plain finish was retained. In this room were to study Karl Marx, V. I. Lenin (who signed in under the alias of Joseph Richter in 1902), G. B. Shaw, Thomas Hardy, Rudyard Kipling, the dancer Isadora Duncan and many others, including the gentleman recorded as 'smoking in a closet', the early Japanese sociologist twice ejected for fighting, the gentleman who blew his nose loudly every half-hour and the cleric who undetected removed entire sermons from *The Pulpit* for the edification of his flock.

At this time the Trustees made an early essay into the up-and-coming field of photography. In 1854 Roger Fenton (later to become famous for his photographs of the Crimean War) was installed in a newly constructed wooden 'photographic house' designed by Sydney Smirke and placed on the Museum roof. Following the Crimean War interlude Fenton returned to the Museum in 1856. Two years later, the Trustees concluded that he was an expensive luxury and the work was abandoned for the time being. Fenton left behind an album of superbly photographed (given the conditions of the time) pictures of busts and the gorilla skeletons. A permanent force of photographers was not set up until 1927.

In 1856–7 the Museum acquired the major part of the remains of the Mausoleum of Halicarnassus in Asia Minor, one of the seven wonders of the ancient world. The site was identified and excavated by C. T. (later Sir Charles) Newton, later appointed Keeper of Greek and Roman Antiquities. These were the first English classical excavations of any importance as scholars' interest turned towards studying objects in context. The sculptures were first housed in temporary wooden sheds on the Colonnade.

Hoa Hakananai'a from
Easter Island,
presented by Queen
Victoria in 1869.

STATUE OF
HOA-HAKA-NANA-IA.
EASTER ISLAND.
PRESENTED BY H.M. THE QUEEN. 1869.
BROUGHT HOME BY H.M.S. TOPAZE.

In June 1860 the eighty-year-old Keeper of Antiquities, Edward Hawkins, resigned.
This provided an opportune moment to break up his unwieldy department which
embraced, *inter alia*, a bewildering combination of coins, ethnography, Egyptian
mummies, Greek marbles and Assyrian bulls. The new division reflected the Victorians'
sense of priorities: the three new departments were Greek and Roman Antiquities,
Coins and Medals and Oriental Antiquities which latter, in spite of its name, included
British and Medieval Antiquities, Ethnography, Egyptian and Assyrian Antiquities.

Panizzi still nursed the hope that the collections might be limited to classical and pagan art which could usefully employ the space taken up 'by what are called British or Irish Antiquities and by the ethnological collection'. Of the latter he observed: 'It does not seem right that such valuable space should be taken up by Esquimaux dresses, canoes and hideous feather idols, broken flints and so on'. The Trustees agreed and no money was spent on purchases.

In spite of the Museum's inevitable chronic lack of space the collections went on growing; it was pilloried in *The Standard* (18 April 1860):

Already if the Overcrowded Lodging House Act could apply to inanimate objects would the Trustees of the British Museum come under the notice of the police, and it continues to be besieged by fresh tenants, to whom it can only offer the door step or a shakedown beneath a temporary shed.

Felix Slade's important collection of glass and drawings came to the Museum by bequest in 1868. The gift amounted to some 950 specimens of ancient glass representing the development of glass manufacture. In the same year the eleven foot high Hoa Hakananai'a, a fine example of sculpture from Easter Island, was collected during the visit of HMS *Topaze*, and presented by the Lords of the Admiralty to Queen Victoria who gave it to the British Museum the following year. A smaller example also acquired on the same voyage was donated directly by the Admiralty. One of the Museum's greatest purchases – the Esquiline Treasure – was acquired in 1866. This silver toilet service of Projecta, a Roman bride, was discovered in a vault in Rome in 1793 and had formed part of the collections of the ducs de Blacas which were bought for £48,000.

Archaeology had expanded and excavations were taking place throughout the classical world. John Turtle Wood excavated the ruins of the Temple of Ephesus between 1863 and 1875 and in the 1860s the Museum supported excavations in Cyrenaica and at Sardis, Rhodes and Halicarnassus (Bodrum). In the second half of the nineteenth century Hormuzd Rassam, Layard's former assistant, and William Kennett Loftus continued the excavations in Assyria, principally at Nineveh. The eccentric George Smith was responsible in 1872 for the discovery in the Museum's collections of an Assyrian tablet giving part of an account of a flood similar to the biblical Deluge. This caught the public imagination and he was despatched to Mesopotamia at the expense of the *Daily Telegraph* where, by amazing good fortune, he found a further fragment describing the flood legend. Smith was sent abroad on two further missions but died in Aleppo in 1876.

Important purchases continued to be made. In 1872 the finest specimens of Greek and Roman coins in the Wigan collection were purchased for £10,000. Two collections of gold ornaments, bronzes and other antiquities were acquired from Mr Alessandro Castellani in 1872–3. Over the period 1880–91 were purchased a series of antiquities from the Earl of Carlisle, which included the superb collection of engraved gems amassed by Henry Howard, fourth Earl of Carlisle (1694–1758). During these years the Roman silver found at Chaourse in France in 1883 and including thirty-six vases, bowls, a handsome ewer and a wine strainer, was also acquired in two instalments.

In the 1880s came the first major break in the collections – the removal of the natural history specimens to a new site on the exhibition grounds at South Kensington. When the proposal had been put forward in the 1860s it had been strongly resisted by Parliament and the public but was favoured by Panizzi, who fervently hoped that with

Giant Irish deer photographed in 1875 prior to the removal of the natural history collections to South Kensington. This gallery, at the top of the North West staircase, is now occupied by Egyptian mummies and coffins.

the natural history collections would go the children who shouted and scampered about in a very improper manner, annoying their elders by eating oranges and throwing the peel about. The new building, designed by Alfred Waterhouse, was begun in 1873 and the mineralogical, geological and botanical collections left in 1880. The new museum opened officially the following year although the Trustees decreed that there should be no formal opening ceremony. The Zoological Department with its 'stuffed tigers and medicated bird skins' left Bloomsbury in 1883. *Punch* some years before had celebrated their forthcoming departure in verse:

> Mother Nature, beat retreat
> Out, M'm, from Great Russell Street.
> Here, in future, folks shall scan
> Nothing but the works of Man.

Holiday Time, 1873. The natural history galleries were the most popular. Sir Henry Ellis had earlier warned against the admission of 'sailors from the dockyards and their girls' (right). *Illustrated London News*.

40

The South Kensington collections as the British Museum (Natural History) remained under the direct control of the British Museum Trustees until a separate board was constituted in 1963.

This departure was a windfall to the antiquities departments who were able to take over the vacant galleries. In 1883 the remains of the Mausoleum of Halicarnassus were at last displayed in a magnificent new gallery constructed parallel to the main western gallery with the aid of money from the White bequest.

In 1879 the Trustees' remaining collection of oil-paintings was further denuded when British notables were transferred to the National Portrait Gallery. This left a rather heterogeneous selection consisting largely of Principal Librarians, Benefactors and Foreigners. Amongst the latter, still to be found in the offices and other rooms throughout the Museum, are an ill-assorted group – Voltaire, Augustus II Elector of Saxony, Martin Luther, Isabella Infanta of Spain, Woureddy (a native of Tasmania) and an enigmatic Italian duo one of whom was thought to be Cosimo de' Medici.

The growth of antiquities in the Museum other than the narrowly 'classical' in the last quarter of the nineteenth century was dominated by the activities of Augustus Wollaston Franks, the virtual creator of the collections of the Department of British and Medieval Antiquities. As late as the mid-nineteenth century the Trustees had expressed to the Royal Commission a distinct disinterest in British antiquities. There were British antiquities on display but these were not to the taste of the general public and were in any case thought to represent a particularly miserable, uncultured group of people best known for dressing in woad and living in holes in the ground, a tribe which had only been redeemed by the coming of classical civilisation with the Romans. Little distinction was made, or understood, between Celtic, Roman and Saxon material.

Small but articulate pressure groups of archaeologists outside the Museum had begun to agitate for more respect to be given to national antiquities and for them to be collected and displayed in a logical manner – a demand supported by the Royal Commission of 1849–50. Hawkins, the elderly keeper in charge of the entire antiquities

Sir Augustus Wollaston Franks KCB FSA (1826–97), virtual creator of many of the present Departments of the Museum. Engraving by Sherbourne for a bookplate in the Society of Antiquaries.

THE ZOOLOGICAL FAMILY REMOVING FROM THE BRITISH MUSEUM TO THEIR NEW HOUSE IN SOUTH KENSINGTON.

'Out with weazles, ferrets, skunks, Elephants, come, pack your trunks' (*Punch*). *The Comic News* in 1861 foresees the departure of the natural history collections from Bloomsbury.

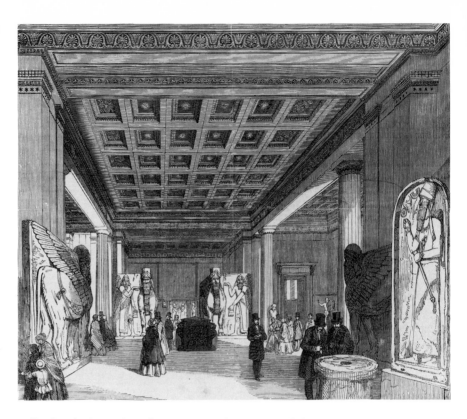

collection, had promised the Trustees as long ago as 1828 to reserve a room in the new buildings exclusively for British antiquities. The project had become more pressing since in 1845 this had been a condition of the offer by Lord Prudhoe of the great collection of ornamental bronzes discovered at Stanwick. Franks was, therefore, appointed in 1851 at the age of twenty-five with specific responsibility for British and Medieval material. His task was eased in 1860 when the still unwieldy, but slightly less complex grouping of Ethnography, British Antiquities and Medieval Antiquities was recognised as a sub-department, at first lodged with Oriental Antiquities (which included the Egyptian and Assyrian material). In 1866 the separate department of British and Medieval Antiquities and Ethnography was born. Thereafter there was considerable progress. Franks and an outsider, John Mitchell Kemble, propounded the view and produced the evidence to show that the early inhabitants of the British Isles were not contemptible savages but craftsmen skilled in enamelling and metal-work, and possessors of a thrilling and unusual decorative style.

During his lifetime Franks made many important donations to the Museum and engineered amazing gifts and purchases by the Trustees. One of the most important of these donations was a unique whalebone casket carved in the 'golden age' of Northumbria, *c.* AD 700, which bears Franks's name. It was found at Auzun in France and donated to the British Museum (save for one side now in the Bargello at Florence). Franks was also responsible for the acquisition in 1892 of the fourteenth-century Royal Gold Cup of the Sovereigns of France and England. The cup is made of solid gold, weighs over four pounds and is ornamented with scenes from the life of St Agnes. Its ownership can be traced back through a number of English sovereigns to John, Duke

An Ethnography gallery at the beginning of the twentieth century typifies Victorian concepts of display.

of Bedford, Regent of France. It was given to a Spanish delegation by James I in 1604 and surfaced at a Spanish convent from which it was purchased by a French collector in 1883. It then passed to a firm of London dealers who offered it to the British Museum at cost (£8,000). The Treasury offered £2,000 and Franks had raised £4,000 by subscription when the dealer died. Franks, a man of some private means, purchased the cup on behalf of the Museum out of his own pocket and continued to receive subscriptions towards the balance.

Franks laid the basis of the Chinese and Japanese collections and ensured that the Museum would be the first in Europe to admit the East as a field suitable for archaeological and art historical research. He developed an already fine collection of Islamic art, arranged for the acquisition of the largest collection of Indian sculpture in Britain in private hands in 1872, the transfer of the collections of antiquities and sculptures originally acquired by the East India Company. These included the sculptures from the great stupa at Amaravati.

He was also responsible for the acquisition of some 10,000 items in the Christy collection of prehistory and ethnography. Henry Christy, a hatter by trade, started to travel in 1850 at the age of forty. His journeys included Cuba, Turkey (whence he introduced towelling into Britain), Asia, Mexico and Hudson's Bay. On his death he left all his collections, with the exception of some French material returned to France, to four trustees, including Franks, together with a considerable sum of money to augment his bequest after his death. From Christy the Museum gained most of its collection of Mexican turquoise masks and other regalia thought to have been part of the placatory gift from the Aztec ruler Montezuma to Emperor Charles V in the early sixteenth century. That same year, 1892, Franks was elected President of the Society of Antiquaries, thus becoming an official Trustee of the British Museum while still a serving member of the staff. Franks's own collections, which he bequeathed to the Museum, comprised finger-rings (over 3,000), drinking vessels, plate, continental porcelain, Japanese netsuke and sword guards and a collection of book plates. The bequest included the magnificent Oxus treasure which had been found in Central Asia at or near the River Oxus in 1877, was carried off by bandits, surfaced in the bazaars of Rawalpindi where the greater part was acquired by General Sir Alexander Cunningham, who sold it to Franks, who had himself bought individual items.

Amongst the staff at this period was an unusual character – Henry Hook VC, one of the survivors of the siege of Rorke's Drift where in 1879 a force of just over a hundred men of the 2nd Battalion 24th Regiment of Foot held off two Zulu impis, an engagement which resulted in eleven Victoria Crosses being awarded – the greatest number in any one engagement. Hook was appointed to the permanent position of 'inside duster' (of the sculptures) on recommendations from one of the commanders at Rorke's Drift (Gonville Bromhead), the leader of the British column, Lord Chelmsford, and the Prince of Wales (through his private secretary). Later he was promoted to take charge of readers' umbrellas and stayed at the Museum until 1904 when he resigned because of ill health.

Another character was the Accountant, Cleeve, who joined in Panizzi's time. Cleeve's holidays were said to be spent partly in examining Borough Treasurer's accounts in seaside towns, and his domestic affairs were so arranged on Civil Service lines that when asked for money by any of his sons he could turn to his ledgers and inform the claimant exactly how much he had cost since birth. In the days before there was any artificial light in the building it is said that Cleeve had stayed on to finish some figures, and could only do it lying on the floor and using the light from the dying fire in the clerks' passage-room outside the Principal Librarian's Room. Panizzi, striding out, fell over the prostrate body of the Accountant who was too deep in calculations to notice his approach. 'Damn you, Mr Cleeve', cried the Principal Librarian, 'you must not be so zealous'.

The next addition to the Museum was the White Wing (1880–4, architect Sir John Taylor) which was built in what was then the Director's back garden. Funds to construct this wing came from the estate of William White, who had lived in the vicinity of Montagu House and was appalled by its ruinous, cramped condition. White, who died in 1823, suggested that his bequest be used for an extension and asked modestly that at some point on the new building the words 'Gulielmus White, Arm. Britt. dicavit 18__' be carved, 'or words to that import' adding, apologetically: 'It is a little vanity of no harm, and may tempt others to follow my example in thinking more of the nation and less of themselves'. The bequest was, however, subject to a life interest by his widow which expired only in 1879. It fell into the Trustees' hands at an opportune moment nevertheless, since the Government was then spending large sums on the new building for the natural history departments and was deaf to appeals for further accommodation at Bloomsbury. (An inscription recording White's gift can be seen on the Montague Street front of the White Wing). White's bequest (£72,000 less £16,300 legacy duty) also provided the Museum with the Mausoleum Room to house the sculptures from Halicarnassus which had been languishing behind glass screens on the Colonnade, and a new boiler house.

An expanded public restaurant off the Egyptian Gallery in 1887 replaced an earlier

ill-omened establishment, opened in 1865 in the basement and closed in 1870 after complaints from both staff and public. A letter on the latter irately protests that portions had dropped from two potatoes to one and that teetotal readers were experiencing great difficulty getting served as the Restaurant rang with joyous cries ordering Irish whiskey, port, brandy and water and wine.

The British Museum was one of the first public buildings in the capital to install electric light. Experiments were carried out in 1879 and 1880, the Trustees being somewhat alarmed when carbon dropped from an open bulb and nearly set fire to the Reading Room. Gas lighting had been provided in the courtyard as long ago as 1818. It had been carried surreptitiously from here into the staff residences – a dangerous practice which did not come to the notice of the horrified Trustees until 1847. The new electric lighting was installed by January 1890 and so pleased were the Trustees that they held a special inspection at 4.30 pm on the afternoon of 15 January and arranged a private view for the public from 5 to 7 pm on the 28th.

Another modern innovation was the removal of many restrictions on visitors who until 1878 were only admitted on Mondays, Wednesdays, Fridays and Saturdays and were not permitted to bring babies in arms. Sunday remained a closed day until 1896.

The period from 1890 to the outbreak of the First World War was one of continued activity and the man who propelled the British Museum into the twentieth century was E. Maunde Thompson, a formidable man, tall, with an eagle face, white beard and piercing blue eyes. Thompson was a distinguished palaeographer, historical scholar and administrator, who from 1898 was the first to hold the title 'Director and Principal Librarian' in recognition of the complexity of administering an institution such as the British Museum. Although he retired in 1909 his retirement lasted until 1929 when he died at the age of ninety. (This advanced age is by no means unusual for a Director of the British Museum, a post which appears to be conducive to longevity. With three exceptions (one of whom died at seventy-six) all Directors have survived to over eighty.) Thompson insisted on strict discipline, which included the wearing of top hats by senior staff in all public galleries except the Reading Room and an absolute prohibition on the riding of bicycles in the public streets.

One of the most important additions to the collections during this period was the Rothschild Bequest. Baron Ferdinand de Rothschild MP, a Trustee, bequeathed a splendid collection of Renaissance *objets d'art* of the finest quality from the new smoking room in his house at Waddesdon in Buckinghamshire on condition that the collection should be exhibited apart from the other collections of the Museum in a room to be called the 'Waddesdon Bequest Room'. Although the location has changed the donor's wishes have been observed.

In 1895 the Trustees, under Act of Parliament, purchased from the Bedford Estate the 69 surrounding houses and $5\frac{1}{2}$ acres of land at a cost of £200,000, thereby gaining possession of the British Museum 'island' for future expansion. Their domain was now bounded by Great Russell Street, Bloomsbury Street and Bedford Square, Montague Place and Montague Street. For once, funds were available for expansion – a £50,000 bequest from Vincent Stuckey Lean and later a grant from the Treasury for £150,000. Lean was a member of a Bristol banking family, he appears to have been unknown to the obituary columns of *The Times* or the *Dictionary of National Biography*, his life having been devoted to a study of the proverbs of all nations. He divided his time between the Reading Room and the Middle Temple (he was a non-practising barrister). His money came from judicious investments and by his will of 1886 and codicil of 1893 he gave to the Trustees the sum of £50,000 which he requested them to appropriate at their discretion to the improvement and extension of library and Reading Room.

An architect, John James Burnet (1859–1938), was commissioned in 1903 to provide an extension to the building. He produced a grandiose scheme for expansion on all four sides over the entire British Museum 'island'. His plans entailed an approach from the north via a broad avenue (now built on by the University of London) and with this in mind Burnet incorporated a reviewing dais at the first-floor central window of the new building. Burnet's full scheme was never realised and sadly this was for almost sixty years the end of the Museum's plans for expansion. The foundation stone of the new building to the north was laid in 1907 by Edward VII but by the time it was opened in May 1914 the old King was dead and the First World War was about to break out. The opening ceremony was sombre. Guests were advised that they need not wear mourning but that they should avoid bright colours. The Trustees never again had both funds and opportunity to develop as they wished – the other houses on the site became subject to preservation orders and the prime site to the north was acquired by the University of London, with which the Museum had long had close associations. Some relaxation of the space problems was however obtained by the move of the newspaper collections to Colindale in north London in 1905.

During Thompson's reign the British Museum was active in excavations in Mesopotamia, Asia Minor, Cyprus and Egypt. Officers of the Museum were sent out on frequent missions to dig at Nineveh and to complete the study of the Behistun Inscription; others visited Egypt to collect antiquities or were lent to the Egypt Exploration Fund to conduct excavations. Excavations were carried out at Ephesus by D. G. Hogarth.

The large totem pole from Queen Charlotte Island now wedged in the North East

Staircase of the Museum was purchased in 1903 from a Dr Newcombe. The freight and carriage of £36. 8s. 6d. exceeded the cost of the pole (£35).

Thompson was succeeded by Sir Frederic Kenyon in 1909. Kenyon's connections with the Museum, like those of many of the staff at that time, went back many years, his mother being the only daughter of Edward Hawkins, second Keeper of Antiquities. Kenyon's daughter, the late Dame Kathleen Kenyon, continued this tradition as a Trustee from 1965 to 1978.

More attention was given to the expanding demand for public services by the appointment of an Official Guide to conduct parties round the Museum and to point out and explain the most interesting objects. This was a typical Museum reversion to the past but, from the numbers attending this voluntary tour it, would appear that the public were better treated than visitors in the eighteenth century. According to the list of rules issued at the time it seems that, while popular, the lectures were subject to a certain amount of interruption from passers-by. In a somewhat involved notice the Director's Office laid down an intriguing rule that 'For the purpose of these rules the Egyptian Gallery and the King's Library shall each be regarded as two rooms divided by a line drawn across the middle'. In 1912 in order to 'widen the influence and increase the interest of the Museum' a sales counter was established in the Entrance Hall for the sale of official publications and postcards.

Immediately prior to the outbreak of war the British Museum was again active in the Middle East. An expedition to Carchemish (a site sixty miles north-west of

The Corridor or Roman Gallery in 1857, 'a noble apartment of lofty dimensions', now forming part of the publications sales area.

Aleppo) was mounted in 1910. Although the site had been previously abandoned in 1878 the progress of the German-financed Berlin-Baghdad railway to the Euphrates more than coincidentally sparked off renewed interest in Hittite archaeology. The dig was organised by D. G. Hogarth, work on the site during 1912–14 being carried out by Leonard Woolley and T. E. Lawrence (of Arabia).

The Trustees became alarmed for the safety of the collections during the pre-War suffragette agitation and insisted that women should only be admitted provided a man would stand surety for their good behaviour. In spite of these precautions and the fact that additional plain clothes police were stationed in the galleries one lady broke a number of panes of glass in the Asiatic Saloon with a chopper and a further onslaught was made with a hatchet on a case in the first Egyptian Room, the latter culprit having been trailed to the spot by the plain clothes police. (Since 1855 regular police officers, paid by the Trustees, had replaced the two watchmen, one of whom locked and unlocked the entrance gate whilst the other went round the museum with a stick and lantern calling the hour. The military guard was discontinued in 1863. The police protected the Museum until 1925 when they were replaced by police pensioners.)

The Museum was to suffer only minimal damage during the First World War – a fragment of spent anti-aircraft shell entered the Iron Library and damaged two books. Shortly after the outbreak of war in 1914 a large number of the more portable objects of special value were removed to greater safety in safes or strong rooms and their places taken by facsimiles or objects of lesser value. The Director, Sir Frederic Kenyon, a member of the Territorial Army, departed for France from where, much to his chagrin, he was recalled. Although he remained in the Army he was also obliged to concern himself with the affairs of the Museum.

In time virtually all the fit male staff of military age disappeared, thereby paving the way for the introduction of female attendants into the Reading Room. As the war progressed more of the collections were removed – at the end of 1917 when serious air raids were expected the most important portable antiquities (including the Parthenon Frieze, the best Greek vases and bronzes, the major Assyrian reliefs, the Rosetta Stone, the finest objects of medieval art and practically the whole collection of coins and medals) were transferred to a station on the newly completed Postal Tube Railway some fifty feet below the surface of Holborn. Printed books, manuscripts and prints and drawings went in fifteen van loads to the National Library of Wales in their new buildings at Aberystwyth. A small selection of exceptionally valuable printed material was housed in the strong room of a country house near Malvern. The mummies joined the figures from the Pediment of the Parthenon in the basement. The Assyrian bulls, the larger Egyptian sculptures and the metopes of the Parthenon were too heavy to move and were protected *in situ* by sandbags.

In 1916 the Government decided to close all museums and public galleries in London in the interests of economy, although the Reading Room and Manuscripts Students Room remained open. The partial clearance of the galleries was seized upon by the Government as a wonderful opportunity to acquire accommodation for Government Departments, thereby relieving pressure on hotels and other buildings. The proposal to introduce the Air Board into the Museum was fought tooth and nail by the Trustees who feared that the by no means empty building would then present both a legitimate and conspicuous target for attack from the air. The Director even went to the length of haranguing the Cabinet at a meeting in the Cabinet Room in Whitehall. A compromise was reached, the Air Board went elsewhere but the Museum received as lodgers the Statistics Branch of the Medical Research Committee (in the sub-ground floor of the King Edward Building), a section of the Prisoners of War Bureau in charge of the effects of German Prisoners (in the basements) and the Registry of Friendly Societies (in the Departments of Prints and Drawings and Egyptian and Assyrian Antiquities). It was not until 1920 that these unwelcome guests were all winkled out.

The collections returned in 1919 and the galleries were progressively reopened. All the staff, however, did not return from the War, and a memorial to the sixteen men who lost their lives was erected at the Front Entrance in 1921. The inscription:

> They shall not grow old
> As we that are left grow old,
> Age shall not weary them
> Nor the years condemn
> At the going down of the sun
> And in the morning
> We will remember them.

was written by the poet Laurence Binyon (Deputy Keeper in charge of Oriental Prints and Drawings 1909–32 and Keeper of Prints and Drawings 1932–3).

The purchase grant was restored after the War and gifts and bequests increased. Among the items received in 1919 were the Northwick collection of engravings and woodcuts, the Sturge Bequest (25 tons of prehistoric stone implements, which called forth a remark by a later Trustee that one of the distinctions of the post, available nowhere else, was of being able to stand in a basement surrounded by a million flints), Sir John Evans's collection of early British and Celtic coins and the Stein collection (including 231 paintings on silk, paper and linen discovered by Sir Aurel Stein in 1908 in the rock-temple of the Thousand Buddhas at Dunhuang). The inter-war period saw the opening of a new Newspaper Library at Colindale, in North London, to provide access to the newspaper collections which had been moved there in 1905.

In 1921 the unwieldy Department of British and Medieval Antiquities and Ethnography was split. Ethnography, Oriental and Occidental ceramics were combined in a separate department. The Far Eastern collections were not yet recognised as having the same stature as European and Middle Eastern material.

It was not until 1933 that a further confusing upheaval took place on the formation of a Department of Oriental Art and Antiquities, with a sub-department of Ethnography which now relinquished oriental sculpture to its senior partner.

Excavations were resumed in the Middle East. During the winter of 1918–19 work started up at Ur, Eridu and al'Ubaid. In 1922 after a gap because of lack of funds the University Museum of Pennsylvania joined with the British Museum on an expedition to Ur under the direction of Leonard Woolley. In 1927 Woolley uncovered a series of graves which came to be called 'The Royal Cemetery'. Here in tombs of the third millennium lay the bodies of guards, ladies-in-waiting and other attendants, the ladies adorned with elaborate head-dresses of gold, lapis lazuli and cornelian. It is said that until he began to make notable finds Woolley had great difficulty in raising funds and was obliged to link as much as possible, and sometimes the impossible, with the Old Testament. His discovery of a flood level at Ur was therefore very providential indeed.

Many items in the Museum's collections had been found on their return from wartime storage to have deteriorated because of the underground environment. The Trustees therefore decided to request the government Department of Scientific and

The arrival of the Assyrian reliefs provoked considerable interest.

49

Industrial Research to report on their condition and offer assistance in restoration and preservation. Dr Alexander Scott FRS, agreed to direct the necessary investigations and put forward a proposal for the establishment of a laboratory in the British Museum. This was sanctioned as a short term experiment for three years and in 1920 a laboratory was set up in 39 Russell Square. Its work was so successful that it was made permanent and eventually taken over by the Trustees in 1931. Scott was succeeded by Dr H. J. Plenderleith in 1933 (to 1959).

In 1923 the Museum attracted its millionth visitor in a year – the first occasion since the Great Exhibition of 1851 (when 2,527,216 visitors descended on the building.) The increase in interest in museums was partly sparked off by Howard Carter's discovery of the tomb of Tutankhamun. This attendance was maintained by the attraction of the British Empire Exhibition the following year, the great Ur Exhibition (with its unbeatable combination of the Bible, human sacrifice and gold) in 1928 and 1929. The forecourt, entrance hall and Egyptian galleries of the period can still be seen as the background to the 'chase scenes' in Britain's first talking picture – Alfred Hitchcock's *Blackmail.*

In 1933 the *Codex Sinaiticus*, the earliest complete New Testament in Greek, was purchased from the Soviet Government for £100,000 and pushed up attendances. Over two-thirds of the price was raised by public subscription. The then Secretary of the Museum writes that 'on the day when at last it was "incorporated" Museum property and on view, there was a crowd of unexampled size and enthusiasm so that the Director was described as a lion thrown to the Christians'. In 1929 the obituary of one of the Museum's great characters – Mike – was inserted in the *Evening Standard* by no less a personage than the retired Keeper of Egyptian and Assyrian Antiquities, Sir Wallis Budge. Mike, from his photographs a rather bedraggled tabby cat, was rather appropriately adopted by the Keeper of Egyptian cat mummies about 1908/10. He preferred to live in the lodge to the west of the Main Gate whence he sallied forth to attack dogs and pigeons. Budge writes of him:

His friendships were few, and he disliked the attentions of strangers, especially the pokings in his ribs which ladies bestowed upon him with their parasols. As for being stroked – many a fair hand has had its glove ripped up by a swift stroke of Mike's claws.

Budge, who joined the staff in 1883, was one of the great augmentors of the Museum collections, his acquisitions during a long Museum career including the Hunters Palette, the Battlefield Palette, the Book of the Dead of Ani, and the predynastic body known as 'Ginger'.

One of the Museum's most singular stories, which had a great vogue at this period, is of a coffin lid (no. 22542, now in the Second Egyptian Room) held by many people to be responsible for the sinking of the *Titanic*. The series of misunderstandings leading to this strange affair is summarised in a disclaimer, into which creeps a note of desperation, put out by Sir Wallis Budge in 1934. The coffin lid's unfortunate reputation grew and flourished from a cycle of misunderstandings – the tale of a mummy case brought to England by a lady, the arrival of which coincided with great destruction of crockery in her home; the presentation to the British Museum of the coffin lid of a chantress of Amen-Ra; and the proposal by a group of people to hold a seance to remove the tormented expression said to be visible in the eyes of the chantress. Publicity about the seance merged with other wild tales and then became transmuted into a legend that, following considerable death and destruction in the British Museum, the Keeper of Egyptian Antiquities sold the coffin lid to an American who transported his new purchase on the *Titanic* thereby occasioning that vessel's collision with an iceberg. Although a large proportion of the passengers perished, the coffin lid was said to have obtained a place in a lifeboat and gone on to spread calamities in the United States and Canada before sinking the *Empress of Ireland* and ending up at the bottom of the St Lawrence River. In an attempt to convey the correct facts Budge states:

The British Museum never possessed either mummy or coffin or cover which did such things . . . The Trustees have no power to sell any object under their charge . . . I did not sell the cover to an American. The cover never went on the Titanic. It never went to America. It was not sold to anybody in Canada, and it is still in the First Egyptian Room in the British Museum . . .

It was, however, too good a story to die. The disclaimer is still being handed out to disbelievers in the official version.

In 1931 the first non-librarian since the eighteenth century to hold the Directorship was appointed. George Francis Hill had been Keeper of Coins and Medals since 1912. He inherited from his predecessor the difficult task of negotiating with the dealer and patron Lord Duveen, who had presented £150,000 to provide a worthy home for the Elgin marbles. Somewhat delicate negotiations took place over the design, for Duveen, although possessing fine artistic taste, had little knowledge of archaeology and there arose a conflict over the claims of the Parthenon sculptures and the design of the building. Duveen is said to have had 'a curious, machine-gun like and hypnotising way of talking, assuming your agreement with what he was saying, which needed real knowledge to stand up to'. However, a compromise was reached and the Museum received a desperately needed new gallery. The architect on this occasion was John Russell Pope of New York, designer of the Jefferson Memorial and the National Gallery of Art in Washington. The gallery was completed in 1938. It was scheduled to open the following year but because of the intervention of war it was to be over twenty years before Duveen's dream was realised.

Above The great marble figure of Amitābha Buddha (China, Sui dynasty), presented in 1938, now presides over the North Staircase of the King Edward VII Building.

Above right The final stages of the Sutton Hoo excavation, 1939.

Towards the end of 1934 Mr George Eumorfopoulos offered his collection of Chinese antiquities, the most extensive and best chosen of all the great private collections being built up in the first part of the twentieth century. The offer was exceedingly generous – items valued at a quarter of a million pounds for £100,000. The Trustees, however, were still financially embarrassed by the purchase of the *Codex Sinaiticus* and made a joint effort with the Victoria and Albert Museum, the British Museum acquiring something less than half of the collection.

The large Amitābha Buddha, now rising through the Edward VII Staircase, was presented in 1938 to commemorate the great International Exhibition of Chinese Art at the Royal Academy in the winter of 1935–6. Like the totem pole, this has not been the easiest of objects to house. For some years it stood in the Front Hall. In 1976, after a period in store, it was manhandled through the large staircase window and deposited in its present position.

In 1938 a Mrs Edith Pretty, encouraged, it is said, by an old man living on her Suffolk estate who, perhaps from folk memory, spoke of a fabulous treasure lying under a series of barrows, persuaded a local archaeologist to excavate. Minor discoveries were made but the second season in 1939 led to the Museum acquiring what the then Keeper of British and Medieval Antiquities described as the most munificent and magnificent single gift ever made in the lifetime of a donor, namely the early seventh-century treasures from the Anglo-Saxon ship burial site at Sutton Hoo. The ship, whose form could be clearly traced, though her timbers were nothing but blackened sand in which the iron nails remained, was 84 feet long and 14 feet in the beam. This find was a revelation of a new pagan Saxon art and archaeology in England, 'an archaeological glory illuminating and confirming the historical fact of a dawning political ascendancy' in the independent Golden Age of East Anglia.

The collection included Early Christian and Byzantine silver objects from the Mediterranean, Merovingian coins from the Continent, hanging bowls of Celtic origin, a helmet and shield from Sweden and, of local origin, jewels and sword fittings set with garnets, a purse, shoulder-clasps and pyramids set with glass mosaic and a great gold buckle. At a coroner's inquest held on 14 August 1939 these objects were found to have been deliberately abandoned with no intention of recovery and therefore not treasure trove (which, as the property of the Crown, would have come to the British Museum in return for an *ex gratia* payment). By Wednesday, 23 August the landowner, Mrs Edith Pretty, had reached a decision and the entire hoard was presented to the British Museum. The treasure had hardly reached the British Museum before it was hurriedly packed and carried off to a place of safety for the duration of the War.

The wartime dispersal of the Museum's treasures makes a fascinating story. Planning for the evacuation of the nation's art treasures started in 1934 when Lord Harlech (Mr Ormsby-Gore) called a meeting of representatives of the national galleries, museums and libraries at the Office of Works. This may appear a surprisingly early date in view of the subsequent climate of appeasement but there were many who had begun to realise the dangers ahead.

In 1938 the Museum and the National Library of Wales started work on a bombproof tunnel at Aberystwyth; a number of country houses were reserved for the rest of the evacuated collections. Packing cases were stockpiled and details of transport were worked out with the railway companies. Towards the end of August 1939 when war seemed inevitable the first container vans were sent to the Museum. In the late evening of Wednesday 23 August the Home Office gave the order to move. Staff were warned and packing and despatch began at seven the next morning. All easily movable material of first importance, including the whole collection of coins and medals, had been sent away by noon on the following Saturday. Packing and despatch of 100 tons of library material of secondary importance, together with prints and drawings, went on for another week. The removal of the heavier items took longer and the transfer of heavy sculpture to the Aldwych Tube tunnel was a continuous war-time activity. Large stone sculptures were protected by sandbags in the galleries. The Parthenon

Objects being moved to safety outside London or in the Aldwych tube tunnel in August 1939.

frieze, which was in course of arrangement, was placed between the pedestals of the pediment groups and the end walls, and covered with a thick sloping roof of sandbags supported on steel sheets and joists to await removal to the Tube tunnel. Staff were posted to the new repositories but, although the exhibition galleries were closed, the Reading Rooms were reopened and remained so throughout the War.

The evacuation was masterminded by the Director and Principal Librarian, Sir John Forsdyke, a somewhat eccentric personality with a cold blue gimlet eye and a very good sense of humour. At the height of the blitz Forsdyke is said to have been recognisable by wearing a tin hat with the word 'Director' stencilled on it. Forsdyke is also said to have attributed his success in his dealings with the Treasury to one thing only, he knew Cicero's letters by heart. Forsdyke's portrait by Sir Gerald Kelly, and those of his predecessors and successors as Directors and Principal Librarians (with one exception) now hang in the Board Room. For this occasion Forsdyke insisted on being painted in full court dress, a challenge not entirely met by the artist since the gold braid in certain areas appears as a yellow smudge.

In August 1940 a 'suicide' exhibition of duplicate antiquities, casts, models and reproductions was mounted by the Department of British and Medieval Antiquities in the Prehistoric Room and the Central Saloon at the head of the main staircase. This exhibition was designed 'not only for the instruction and entertainment of war-time visitors, but also as a possible sacrifice to the perils of war'. It included some aptly designated 'courageous' labels giving an outline of European prehistory and early history from before 550,000 BC to the Norman Conquest.

The first (of six) high explosive bombs to fall on the Museum arrived through the roof on 18 September 1940. This passed through the Prints and Drawings Students Room, the floor of that room, four other concrete floors and landed in the sub-ground floor. The tail was torn off by a girder and it failed to explode. On 22 September a smaller bomb came through the same hole but got no further than the first mezzanine. As Sir John Forsdyke noted: 'The two bombs that came through the same hole and did not explode deserve special notice as a rare or perhaps unique phenomenon, appropriately occurring in a Museum. But it is, ironically, a phenomenon of which no material evidence can exist'. The following day yet another high explosive bomb fell in the King's Library destroying 150 volumes. On 16 October the Reading Room suffered a narrow escape when an oil bomb dropped through the dome. This fortunately shed its burning oil outside on the copper sheathing of the roof where it was extinguished by the Museum firemen. If it had burst inside it would have destroyed the room. Later that month the now empty Duveen Gallery was hit by a small bomb which caused a fair amount of damage to the interior. In the same raid the storage block of the Newspaper Library at Colindale was destroyed and with it 30,000 volumes, mostly of nineteenth-century British provincial newspapers.

The Museum had been relatively fortunate, but on 10 May 1941 its luck ran out as dozens of incendiaries fell and the resulting fires spread in the space between the old copper roofs and the ceilings. The roofs of the Roman Britain Room, the Central Saloon and adjoining Prehistoric Room, the main staircase, the Room of Greek and Roman Life and its annexes, the Medal Room, the Greek Bronze Room, and the First Vase Room were destroyed. The 'suicide' exhibition fulfilled its destiny. In the south-west quadrant of the general library 250,000 books were lost, the water from the fire hoses ruining most of those that survived the flames.

The Central Saloon
after the air raid of May
1941. Little remains of
the 'suicide exhibition'.

The events of this memorable night are recounted laconically in a letter from the
Museum Secretary to one of the out-stations. Having first pointed out that fares may
be paid for staff from the out-stations visiting their homes in the country if the cost did
not exceed journeys to London, then accusingly noting that the amount of soap used
was more than at other out-stations and that therefore demands must be diminished,
the writer enclosed as a consolation a packet of economy labels. Only then, in passing,
does he mention 'the bad time we had on Saturday night last'.

On 24 April 1946 the British Museum at last reopened some of its galleries to the
public although it was many years before the damage was repaired. (The building is
still, in 1985, protected in some areas by temporary roofs.)

Forsdyke's successor in 1950 was Sir Thomas Kendrick to whom fell the task of
reopening galleries shut or damaged during the war. Kendrick was a kindly, popular
Director with a passion for a great variety of strange hobbies – for example, collecting
bus tickets and the television programme Z Cars. His academic career encompassed a
bewildering range of subjects; beginning as a prehistorian he travelled through Early
Britain, the Anglo-Saxon and Viking periods, closing with a distinct interest in the
Renaissance; all these by way of the Lisbon earthquake of 1755. It was unfortunate
that because of the outbreak of the Korean War in the year of his appointment he was
unable to put all his plans for the Museum into execution as quickly as he would have
liked.

The Duveen Gallery which should have opened in 1939, remained closed for repairs
and arrangement until 1962 when it was opened by the Archbishop of Canterbury.
The four galleries at the head of the main staircase containing the Prehistoric and
Romano-British collections had to be virtually rebuilt as were the Greek and Roman

55

An Education Service was not established until 1970. The Trustees' prohibition on babes in arms was lifted in 1879 but between the Wars the possibility of banning children deposited for the afternoon by their parents was from time to time discussed. *Illustrated London News.*

Closing Time: The Lost Tribe waiting to be recognised.

Life Room (1960) and the offices of the Department of Coins and Medals (1959). In 1969 fourteen new Greek and Roman galleries were opened and the following year saw the turn of the new Assyrian galleries.

As the decades rolled by, however, the Museum began to look less as described by Sir Mortimer Wheeler in 1960: 'objects in serried lines like an untidy regiment on parade, many unlabelled or not in context, dusty and unloved'. More space was provided by the temporary move of the ethnographic collections to the Museum of Mankind at Burlington Gardens near Piccadilly Circus in 1970. (The importance of these collections had been recognised by the establishment of a Department of Ethnography in 1946.) In 1964 the Department had received its largest single acquisition ever – 15,000 pieces from the Wellcome Foundation. The shortage of space at Bloomsbury became even more acute as throughout the building available nooks and crannies filled with primitive spears, bows and arrows.

In 1955 the former Egyptian and Assyrian Department split in two reflecting the great expansion of the two main subjects of Egyptology and Assyriology – particularly the advances since the First World War in knowledge concerning Mesopotamian, Iranian, Anatolian, Syrian, Palestinian, Arabian and Levantine archaeology and linguistics.

In the fifties the Museum received two magnificent monetary bequests, both with far-reaching effects. In his highly complicated will the dramatist George Bernard Shaw bequeathed one third share of his residuary estate (the other beneficiaries being the Royal Academy of Dramatic Art and the National Gallery of Ireland) 'in acknowledgement of the incalculable value to me of my daily resort to the Reading Room [of the British Museum] at the beginning of my career'. Substantial in any case, this fund was swelled beyond the Museum's wildest dreams by the success of the musical *My Fair Lady*.

Mr P. T. Brooke Sewell, a merchant banker living in Canada, who was interested in Oriental, and particularly Indian, antiquities, gave considerable sums during his lifetime and left a further substantial donation in his will which came to the British Museum following his death in 1958. Mr Brooke Sewell's purpose was to enable the Museum to build up the collections of objects which were to bear his name in perpetuity and in this he succeeded magnificently. The Brooke Sewell fund and bequest have revolutionised and continue to transform the Museum's collections in these fields.

In 1963 a new British Museum Act came into force, replacing that of 1753 and succeeding provisions. The Board of Trustees was slimmed down from 51 (26 *ex officio* including 15 members of the Government, 9 family Trustees, the Royal Trustee, 15 elected by the others) to 25. The Sovereign continues to appoint one Trustee, 15 are provided by the Prime Minister, 5 elected by the Board and one each is nominated by the British Academy, Royal Academy, Royal Society and Society of Antiquaries. Members are no longer appointed for life. The first Chairman was Lord Radcliffe, one of the greatest legal authorities of his generation, whose devastating comments on a wide variety of topics particularly on points of law are now liberally sprinkled amongst the Museum archives, reducing junior members of the Civil Service legal branch to despair.

The Act also permitted the Trustees, under certain conditions, to make loans to exhibitions abroad instead of being obliged to go through the cumbersome procedure of an Act of Parliament, previously used for the loan of Magna Carta to the United

States of America. It also permitted storage of sections of the collection outside the main building. The British Museum (Natural History) at South Kensington was formally separated – a provision which has so far not entirely stemmed the flow of misdirected specimens (maggot-infested birds and unidentified insects) being delivered by mistake to Bloomsbury.

In 1969 division occurred within the antiquities departments when British and Medieval Antiquities, the rump of Franks's old department, split into two – Medieval and Later Antiquities and Prehistoric and Romano-British Antiquities. Dropping the confusing description 'British' from the Medieval Department's title reflected both the actual scope of the collections (which range far outside the British Isles) and the fact that the Museum's reputation was now such that it was no longer considered necessary, as it had been in the nineteenth century, to reassure the public as to the Museum's concern with national antiquities.

The post-war period saw the beginnings of the greatest upheaval in the Museum since the move of the natural history collections to South Kensington in the 1880s. The need for more space for the library had been apparent since the nineteenth century. In 1928 the Royal Commission on National Museums and Galleries had recommended as urgently necessary the provision of more room. In 1943 discussions began on future plans for London. A preservation order was placed on Bedford Square where the Museum had hoped to expand. It was recognised that something must be done as the Library was by now growing at the rate of over a million items a year. In the London County Council's Greater London Development Plan of 1951 the area opposite the front of the building between Great Russell Street and New Oxford Street was designated as the site for the new library. A Public Enquiry into the plan was held in 1952 and in 1955 the Minister of Housing approved the designation in the plan. Architects were appointed in 1962 and their outline scheme approved by Government in 1964. The Ministry of Works began gradually to buy up freeholds on the Bloomsbury site but in 1967 the London Borough of Camden's objections to the plan were upheld by the Government. However, in 1970 the Government reconsidered its decision, again favouring Bloomsbury, provided certain buildings such as Nash's Pharmaceutical Society were preserved. In 1971 a new Government published a White Paper announcing its decision to set up an organisation to be known as the British Library which would take over the three library departments of the British Museum (Printed Books, Oriental Manuscripts and Printed Books, and Western Manuscripts), the National Reference Library for Science and Invention, the National Central Library, the National Lending Library for Science and Technology and the British National Bibliography. The erstwhile Museum departments would be housed in the new buildings to the south of the Museum, connected with the old building by a tunnel. The British Library Act of 1972 sealed this division, leaving the British Museum with the national collections of antiquities, coins and medals, prints and drawings and ethnography.

Bowing to pressure, the Government eventually abandoned their intention of using the Bloomsbury site where there was a residential community and in 1975 it was announced that a new purpose-built library would arise on the site of the potato market near St Pancras station. Five years later the decision was made to start on the scheme with a reduced first stage of the building. The new building has been scheduled to open in 1993 (when the Museum will take over its first accession of Library space). The final departure of all the library departments from Bloomsbury is to take place by the turn of

58

the century.

In 1967 when the Government suddenly made the decision not to build the new library on the Great Russell Street site the Trustees determined to found a society the prime object of which would be to constitute a body of informed opinion about the needs of the British Museum. The Trustees also hoped to raise money to supplement government building grants. The British Museum Society was therefore formally established in 1968. In the event the Society has developed into a group of Friends of the Museum which meets to extend knowledge of the British Museum collections and which from time to time makes donations towards purchases. The Society now includes the categories of Patrons and Associates (established in 1988).

In the 1970s the Trustees moved even further from the limited view expressed by their predecessors a hundred years earlier that: 'the duty of the Trustees is carefully to preserve and efficiently to exhibit the objects entrusted to them . . . they are not in any other sense connected with education'. With wider educational facilities available to the public the restricted services previously provided were insufficient and in 1970 an Educational Services section was established. Children are now welcome as they explore the galleries clutching work sheets and clipboards, the more unscrupulous waylaying warders for assistance in answering questions.

In 1973 the Museum started its own publishing house, British Museum Publications Ltd – a long way from the sellers of 'spurious guides' with whom the Trustees had to contend during the last century. Owned by the Trustees and self-financing, BMP gave the Museum's publications and other allied commercial activities new opportunities for enterprise. The publications now range from the most specialist works of scholarship to books for the popular market, guides, cut-out models and leaflets, most of which are now available through booksellers throughout the world. The Company also is responsible for the well-known range of replicas of objects in the collections, as well as for the shops and sales points in the Museum.

A Design Officer was appointed in 1964. The most popular exhibition in the BM's history – Treasures of Tutankhamun – was held in 1972; 1,694,117 visitors turned up, and queueing for Tutankhamun became the fashion. Although much was made of the Pharoah's curse at the time, on the whole the staff involved with the exhibition appear to have suffered no ill effects. An embarrassing near-disaster occurred, however, when the treasure arrived under conditions of strict security at the south-west gate and it was found that a carelessly parked car was obstructing the entrance. The offending vehicle was bodily lifted by a group of policemen and carried down Great Russell Street. The Vikings exhibition of 1980 attracted almost half a million visitors enlivened by occasional groups in more or less correct representations of Viking costumes.

On 1 January 1974 admission charges were at last imposed, previous attempts in 1784 and 1923 having foundered. They caused problems from the start since the ticket machines installed in the previous December had rusted on the Colonnade. The charges proved expensive to administer and somewhat cumbersome to operate since the Library areas remained free. They were repealed in March; it was impossible fully to assess their effect since they coincided with a crippling strike by coal miners, a consequent series of drastic electricity cuts and a gloomy three-day working week, but attendances for one reason or another fell dramatically.

On the scientific side a marked change took place in the role of the Research Laboratory which had been started in 1931 principally to develop satisfactory methods for the treatment of objects. In 1961 it settled into a purpose-built building and turned

"Hold tight, Grandma, here comes The Curse of Tutankhamun . . . POW!"

to research into the composition and fabrication of antiquities. Among current projects are the study of gilding techniques in antiquity, analysis of Celtic gold coins, research into the feasibility of dating burnt flints from Palaeolithic sites, and the petrological examination of thin sections from ceramics to establish the sources of the raw materials used and gain information on the methods of manufacture. The Research Laboratory is also engaged in the long term computerisation of the records of the Museum's millions of objects.

The practical division within the laboratory between research and the application of conservation techniques was further reinforced by the establishment of a separate Department of Conservation in 1975 with its own research and development section. This service has developed an outstanding position in the application of new techniques and materials to the conservation of antiquities.

As in previous centuries the Museum is continually rearranging its galleries to suit altered public tastes, to exhibit new acquisitions or, on occasions, to prop up the old structure, for Smirke's innovations in cast iron have not entirely stood the test of time. The Museum turned, as previously, to private benefactors as well as to Government for the remodelling of the Egyptian Sculpture Gallery between 1979 and 1981. Some eyebrows were raised at the Trustees' decision to use light colour in place of the dark red Victorian paintwork which emerged when partitions were taken down. However, the Museum was able to produce a letter by the architect Robert Smirke dated 10 August 1833 in which he emphatically stated that he 'would prefer no other colour than that of stone', a plea ignored by later nineteenth-century Trustees when redecorating the gallery. Appropriately, one of the major donors to this scheme was one of England's greatest sculptors, Henry Moore, who was influenced by the BM on arrival in London as a young student in the 1920s, one of his favourite objects being the eighteenth

The Tutankhamun Exhibition of 1972–3, the first 'blockbuster', provided a marvellous opportunity for cartoonists.

Over one hundred years of grime is removed from the Portland stone in 1978. It is probable that, because of London's pollution in the nineteenth century, the façade as we see it today was only visible to the Victorians for a decade or so.

dynasty seated Egyptian official and his wife (Registration no. 36) which is displayed in the new gallery. The resemblance of this statue, and other objects within the Museum, to Mr Moore's subsequent work is unmistakable.

The great Townley collection, wholly consigned below stairs in the 1960s, can again be seen by the public in a lower gallery thanks to the generosity of the Wolfson Foundation.

In 1978 Smirke's Colonnade received a face-lift – the black velvet deposited by a hundred years of London smog has gone and the result is a much more cheerful building which now reflects the different colours of the sun's rays throughout the day.

An addition to the Museum buildings was formally opened by the Secretary of State for the Environment in 1980, having been progressively occupied since the end of 1978. This New Wing, designed by Colin St John Wilson, incorporates a special exhibitions gallery, public and staff restaurants, boardroom, offices and workrooms. It is the first stage of an L-shaped building which has been planned since the early 1960s. An attempt to embellish the Great Russell Street façade with upwards-climbing ivy foundered as the ivy developed a contrary sense of direction.

In the past two decades the collections have been revolutionised as the Museum woke up to the existence of the twentieth century and began to collect frequently in areas ignored by any other institutions. The exhibition 'Collecting the Twentieth Century' held in 1991 summed up these achievements.

In 1986 at a splendid Kikoshki ceremony, using the traditional requirements of wet fish, tree branches and sand, and conducted by a Shinto priest flown in from Japan (there being no practitioner in Europe), work commenced on the conversion of the

space at the top of the King Edward VII building – the largest attic conversion in London. In 1990 the new Japanese Galleries (consisting of the Konica Gallery, the Urasenke Gallery, a lobby donated by Brian and Esther Pilkington and the main gallery built with funds from donors in Japan and the UK, was opened by HIH Prince Fumihito of Japan. Due to the requirements for the oversight of the work on the gallery a separate Department of Japanese Antiquities was set up in 1987.

Of other aspects of the final years of the twentieth century it is not always possible to write with complete candour and accuracy and, as Edward Miller, author of the standard history of the British Museum, once commented, a publisher is faced with a manuscript bearing a closer resemblance to an annual report than to an anecdotal history.

It is, however, possible to look towards the future. The Museum has always relied heavily on private donors for its collections and for much of its building: many of these are listed in the Summary of Events (pp. 66–9). This generosity is again proving vital as the British Library begins to depart and forty per cent of Smirke's building, devoid of books, becomes available to house antiquities and services. The decision having been taken in the 1970s to sell the leases of the area south of the Museum, where sandwich bars now breed, and move the Library to St Pancras, the Museum now has for the first time in its history the opportunity to take over the entire Bloomsbury site. The antiquities sections – the 'cuckoo in the nest' – have now (not without regret) tipped out the other growing nestlings: Natural History and the Library. In 1995 the Museum did manage partially to expand across the road, by acquiring what had previously been the Royal Mail

Sorting Office in New Oxford Street (above the private line used for the storage of antiquities in the First World War). With the assistance of grants from the Heritage Lottery Fund and the Clothworkers' Foundation, this will by 1999 be transformed into a Study Centre and store for the next half century.

The British Museum is an institution uniquely placed to celebrate the Millennium – indeed it is one of the few places in the world with exhibits to illustrate all millennia since the emergence of human material culture. In the centre of the Museum – the Great Court – Sydney Smirke's Round Reading Room will be revealed; within it will be a new Information Centre funded by the Annenberg Foundation. Beneath the courtyard there will be an Education Centre (funded by a number of generous benefactors) and the Sainsbury African Galleries. Soaring above will be a magnificent glass roof; designed by Sir Norman Foster, this and the restoration of the courtyard area is to be funded by a grant from the Millennium Commission.

Thus the Museum began with a lottery and ends its first quarter-millennium with a lottery. The British Museum has always shown a determined capacity for survival as well as the ability to reinvent itself whilst retaining its essential character. It spent much of the mid-nineteenth century as a building site and much of the final quarter of that century desperately concerned at its diminishing finances, but survived to become what it is today.

The staff today profit from, and curse, the activities of their predecessors and, in turn, lay foundations for their successors. The loss of the great characters of the past is lamented in ignorance of the fact that the 'characters' about whom the next century will reminisce are with us today. Their activities must, however, await a future volume of the history of the British Museum.

The King's Library, the oldest surviving part of the Museum building, in 1875. Photograph by Frederick York.

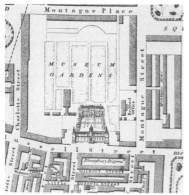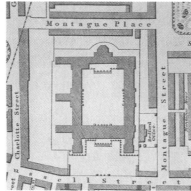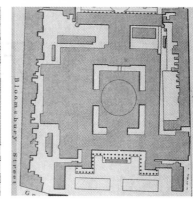

Further Reading

The British Museum, Report of the Trustees, London, Trustees of the British Museum (published triennially since 1966)

The British Museum Quarterly, vol. XVIII, nos 1–4, Trustees of the British Museum, London, 1953

CAYGILL, MARJORIE, *Treasures of the British Museum*, British Museum Press, London, 2nd edition, 1992

CAYGILL, MARJORIE, and CHERRY, JOHN (eds), *A.W. Franks: Nineteenth-Century Collecting and the British Museum*, British Museum Press, London, forthcoming, 1997

COWTAN, ROBERT, *Memories of the British Museum*, Bentley, London, 1872

CROOK, J. MORDAUNT, *The British Museum: a case-study in architectural politics*, Allen Lane, London, 1972

EDWARDS, EDWARD, *Lives of the Founders, and Notices of some Chief Benefactors and Organizers, of the British Museum*, Trubner & Co., London, 1870

ESDAILE, ARUNDELL, *The British Museum Library*, Allen & Unwin, London, 1946

FRANCIS, SIR FRANK (ed.), *Treasures of the British Museum*, Thames & Hudson, London, 1971

GRIFFITHS, ANTONY (ed.), *Landmarks in Print Collecting: Connoisseurs and Donors at the British Museum since 1753*, British Museum Press, London, and Museum of Fine Arts, Houston, 1996

GÜNTHER, A. E., *The Founders of Science at the British Museum, 1753–1900*, Halesworth Press, Suffolk, 1980

JENKINS, IAN, *Archaeologists and Aesthetes: The Sculpture Galleries of the British Museum in the Nineteenth Century*, British Museum Press, London, 1992

MACGREGOR, ARTHUR (ed.), *Sir Hans Sloane: Collector, Scientist, Antiquary*, British Museum Press, London, 1994

MILLER, EDWARD, *That Noble Cabinet: A History of the British Museum*, Deutsch, London, 1973

WILSON, DAVID M., *The British Museum: Purpose and Politics*, British Museum Publications Ltd, London 1989

The steady growth of the Museum building: (left to right) Montagu House purchased in 1754, with Robert Smirke's anticipated plan of 1823 and the Museum site in the mid-twentieth century.

Summary of Major Events in the Museum's History

1753   (11 January) Death of Sir Hans Sloane
(27 January) First meeting of Sloane's Trustees
(19 March) Main Parliamentary debate
(7 June) The British Museum Act receives the royal assent
(11 December) First meeting of the new Board of Trustees appointed
by the Act. 15 additional Trustees elected

1754   Negotiations for the purchase of Montagu House (concluded 1755)

1757   Gift of the Old Royal Library by King George II
Museum gardens opened to the public (by ticket)

1759   (15 January) British Museum opens to the public

1772   Purchase of the Hamilton collection of vases, antiquities and drawings

1799   Bequest of the Cracherode collection

1802   Arrival of the Rosetta Stone and other antiquities ceded under the
Treaty of Alexandria (1801)

1805   Purchase of the first part of the Townley collection; second 1814

1808   Opening of the Townley Gallery (Antiquities), (begun 1804)

1814   Purchase of the Phigaleian marbles (the sculptures from the Temple of
Apollo at Bassae, received 1815)

1816   Elgin Marbles purchased by Parliament and vested 'in perpetuity in the
Trustees of the British Museum'
Temporary building designed by Robert Smirke for the Elgin Marbles
(opened 1817, demolished 1831)

1823   Robert Smirke's plans for the new Museum building presented to the
Trustees and approved

Opening of the King Edward VII Building by King George V and Queen Mary in 1914.

66

The Princess of Wales at the opening of the Wolfson Gallery of Roman Antiquities in June 1991.

	Donation by George IV of George III's 'King's Library'; work on the repository begins 14 July
1824	Bequest of the Payne-Knight collection
1825	Fragments from Persepolis reliefs presented by Sir Gore Ouseley
	Purchase from the widow of Claudius James Rich of his collection of manuscripts, coins and other antiquities made during his travels in Mesopotamia (d. 5 Oct 1821)
1826	Work begins on western gallery
1827	Completion of King's Library; books installed 1828, opened to the public October 1831
1832	New Elgin gallery opened to the public
1833	Work begins on North Wing
1834	Egyptian sculpture installed in north division of West Wing
1836	Establishment of the Department of Prints & Drawings
1841	Excavations commence for South Front
1842	Arrival of first collection of Lycian or Xanthian Marbles excavated by Charles Fellows 1842–44; Second collection received 1844
	Demolition of Montagu House begins, completed 1845
	Part demolition of Townley Gallery; completed 1846
1845	Offer by Lord Prudhoe of Iron Age bronzes from Stanwick
	Austen Henry Layard begins excavations in Assyria; employed by the Trustees from 1846
1847	Opening of New Entrance Hall
	Arrival of the first Assyrian sculptures
1851	Appointment of Augustus Wollaston Franks as Assistant with special responsibility for the British and Medieval collections
1853/4	Excavations at Nineveh and Nimrud (H. Rassam)
1854	Work begins on new Reading Room, completed May 1857
	Egyptian sculptures occupy both divisions of West Wing
1854/6	Excavations at Nineveh (W. K. Loftus)
1856	Purchase of the Roach-Smith collection of British Antiquities

1857-9	Acquisition of the marbles from Halicarnassus and Cnidus excavated by C. T. Newton 1856-9
1860	Retirement of the Keeper of Antiquities, Edward Hawkins
1861	Establishment of the Departments of Oriental Antiquities, Greek and Roman Antiquities, and Coins and Medals
1865	Acquisition of the marbles excavated at Ephesus by Charles Turtle Wood; excavations 1863-74 Bequest of Henry Christy's (d. 4 May) ethnographical collection and setting up of the Christy Fund
1866	Establishment of the Department of British & Medieval Antiquities and Ethnography
1873	Work begins on the British Museum (Natural History) at South Kensington; formally opened 1881; last natural history collections leave Bloomsbury 1883
1877	Extension to the north of the Front Hall
1879	Cash legacy bequeathed by William White (d.1823) becomes available First experiments on the use of electricity in the Reading Room
188?	Acquisition of some of the collections of the India Museum including the Amaravati sculptures
1881	Anderson collection of Japanese and Chinese paintings acquired
1882	Work begins on the White Wing; occupied from July 1885
1890	Museum fully lit by electricity
1894	Purchase of the surrounding properties from the Bedford Estate, negotiations concluded 1895, Treasury loan paid off 1947
1897	Death of Augustus Wollaston Franks (21 May) and bequest of his immense collection (retired 1896)
1904	Work begins on the King Edward VII Building with the aid of a legacy from Vincent Stuckey Lean (d.1899); foundation stone laid 1907
1912-14	Excavations at Carchemish
1914	Opening of the King Edward VII Building by King George V and Queen Mary
1922	Establishment of the Research Laboratory (authorised 1920)
1922-34	Excavations at Ur
1936	Work begins on the Duveen Gallery; funds offered by Lord Duveen 1928; completed 1938; installation of sculptures begins 1939; opened following war damage 1962
1939	Discovery of the great ship burial at Sutton Hoo; donation of the finds by Mrs Edith Pretty (23 August) evacuation of the collections ordered, begins 24 August
1941	(10/11 May) Incendiary raid destroys south-west library quadrant and a number of upper exhibition galleries, students rooms and offices
1946	Establishment of separate Department of Ethnography
1947	Reopening of Print Room and galleries following wartime evacuation
1955	Egyptian & Assyrian splits into Egyptian Antiquities and Western Asiatic Antiquities
1959	Opening of reconstructed Coin Room
1960	Opening of reconstructed Greek & Roman Life Room

Princess Margaret Countess of Snowdon at the opening of the Raymond and Beverly Sackler Galleries of Egypt and Africa and Early Mesopotamia, July 1991.

1963	New British Museum Act; separation of British Museum and British Museum (Natural History)
1968	Opening of reconstructed Prehistoric and Roman Britain galleries British Museum Society founded
1969	Separation of British & Medieval Antiquities into Prehistoric & Romano-British Antiquities and Medieval & Later Antiquities Opening of remodelled ground floor Classical sculpture galleries
1970	Opening of remodelled Assyrian galleries Transfer of Department of Ethnography to Museum of Mankind
1972	British Library Act
1973	(1 July) separation of British Museum and British Library
1975	Work begins on New Wing; occupied from 1978; formally opened 1980
1981	Remodelled Egyptian Sculpture Gallery opened
1985	Opening of Wolfson Galleries of Classical Sculpture and Inscriptions
1988	Opening of A. G. Leventis Gallery of Cypriot Antiquities Scheme for Patrons and Associates established
1989	Opening of John Addis Islamic Gallery
1990	Opening of Japanese Galleries
1991	Opening of Wolfson Gallery of Roman Antiquities; Raymond and Beverly Sackler Galleries of Egypt and Africa and Early Mesopotamia
1992	Opening of Joseph E. Hotung Gallery of Oriental Antiquities; Asahi Shimbun Gallery of Amaravati Sculpture
1993	Opening of Raymond and Beverly Sackler Galleries of Later Mesopotamia, Ancient Anatolia and Early Egypt
1994	Opening of Europe: 15th–18th Centuries (dedicated to Sir Denis Hamilton) and Europe: the 19th Century (in honour of Mr and Mrs T.Y. Chao); Mexican Gallery; Hirayama Conservation Studio Launch of 250th anniversary development programme (Hon. President HRH The Princess Margaret, Countess of Snowdon)
1995	Opening of Hellenistic Gallery (Museums & Galleries Improvement Fund, The Wolfson Family Trust, Mr Samuel Merrin and the A.G. Leventis Foundation)
1997	(January) Opening of HSBC Money Gallery; (summer) opening of Weston Gallery of Roman Britain and gallery of Celtic Europe

'Electric lighting of the British Museum' – artist's impression in the *Illustrated London News*, February 1890 of a 'large and distinguished company' enjoying the new lighting in the Egyptian Sculpture room.

Left One of the new lights.

The Principal Librarians and Directors of the British Museum

(From 1898 onwards 'Director and Principal Librarian'. From 1973 the title was altered to 'Director' with the departure of the library departments)

1756	Gowin Knight, MD
1772	Matthew Maty, MD
1776	Charles Morton, MD
1799	Joseph Planta
1827	Henry Ellis (Sir Henry Ellis, KH)
1856	Antonio Panizzi (Sir Anthony Panizzi, KCB)
1866	John Winter Jones
1873	Edward Augustus Bond (Sir Edward Bond, KCB)
1888	Edward Maunde Thompson (Sir Edward Maunde Thompson, GCB, ISO)
1909	Frederic George Kenyon (Sir Frederic Kenyon, KCB)
1931	George Francis Hill (Sir George Hill, KCB)
1936	Edgar John Forsdyke (Sir John Forsdyke, KCB)
1950	Thomas Downing Kendrick (Sir Thomas Kendrick, KCB)
1959	Frank Chalton Francis (Sir Frank Francis, KCB)
1968	John Frederick Wolfenden (Lord Wolfenden, CBE)
1974	John Wyndham Pope-Hennessy (Sir John Pope-Hennessy, CBE)
1977	David Mackenzie Wilson (Sir David Wilson, Kt)
1992	Robert G. W. Anderson

Index